STATE, COOPERATIVES AND RURAL CHANGE

LUND STUDIES IN GEOGRAPHY
SER. B. HUMAN GEOGRAPHY NO. 53

STATE, COOPERATIVES AND RURAL CHANGE

Edited by

Björn Gyllström
and
Franz-Michael Rundquist

1989
THE ROYAL UNIVERSITY OF LUND
DEPARTMENT OF GEOGRAPHY
LUND UNIVERSITY PRESS

Financial support for this publication has been provided by the Swedish Council for Research in the Humanities and Social Sciences *(HSFR)*, and the Swedish Agency for Research Cooperation with Developing Countries *(SAREC)*.

LUND UNIVERSITY PRESS
BOX 141
S-221 00 LUND
SWEDEN

CHARTWELL-BRATT LTD
OLD ORCHARD, BRICKLEY ROAD
BROMLEY, KENT BR1 2NE
ENGLAND

Art nr 20141

ISBN 0-86238-228-9

ISBN 91-7966-083-5

CONTRIBUTORS

Gyllström, Björn, Department of Social and Economic Geography, University of Lund.

Hatti, Neelambar, Department of Economic History, University of Lund and IMPART Centre, Hyderabad, India.

Holmén, Hans, Department of Social and Economic Geography, University of Lund.

Rundquist, Franz-Michael, Department of Social and Economic Geography, University of Lund.

Ståhl, Michael, SAREC, Swedish Agency for Research Cooperation with Developing Countries, Stockholm.

CONTENTS

INTRODUCTION

From 1983 to 1985, famine in Africa caught public attention throughout the world. However, the recognition that Africa faces a serious and deepening crisis of agricultural production and rural development is not new. Since the early 1960s, African agriculture has been unable to keep pace with population growth. Per capita production has fallen by 20 per cent and half of all African nations are net importers of food (Haque 1987).

The conditions facing small farmers in Africa are as varied and complex as the continent itself and so are the factors underlying the adverse trends of recent decades. Thus, while most countries have been stressing the importance of agriculture, they have in reality pursued trade, exchange rate, fiscal and monetary policies that are strongly biased against primary production. This discrimination is often due to development strategies that promote domestic industries behind high trade barriers. Such import substitution strategies result in internal terms of trade that accelerate the shift of resources out of rural areas, thus discriminating also against agricultural exports and the position of primary produce that compete with imports.

At the same time it is clear that sectoral and rural policies of direct consequence for agricultural production can either mitigate or exacerbate the negative consequences of general economic policies. Thus, many governments try to offset the bias against agricultural producers through institutional reforms, extension services, input subsidies, and marketing services. In these fields, the direct involvement of public agencies and government promotion of cooperatives have been widely accepted as adequate means of supporting the development of smallholder agriculture.

The attention accorded agricultural cooperatives in Africa, both by governments and donor organizations, has no doubt been encouraged by the effectiveness of such organizations in advancing agrarian interests in industrialized countries. To date, however, available research presents a rather bleak picture as regards their contributions to agricultural and rural development in Africa. Thus, cooperatives have been blamed both for a mediocre record in terms of economic performance and for having failed in contributing towards basic social development aspirations (Gyllström 1985).

Explanations to observed shortcomings have largely focussed on the cooperative mode of organization and how it is affected by local social structure. According to this interpretation, parochial relations contained by social networks at the local level thus tend to permeate and jeopardize the management and democratic control of societies.

However, contrary to the impression given by governments and other propagators of cooperatives, the democratic qualities have mostly been absent from the organizational designs applied in Africa. Further, it is likely that the role of the local social environment, with respect to inherent 'traditional forces', has been exaggerated. As pointed out by Peter Worsley,

"When we begin to list the factors which make for or inhibit success (of cooperatives) we begin to realize that to concentrate simply on the question of pre-existing social bonds is wrongly to isolate only one aspect of the problem." *(1971:37).*

Given the attention paid to democratic management and its relations to the social structure of smallholder communities it apparently is assumed that local cooperatives are operating as autonomous establishments. This is not the case. As a matter of fact, it is mostly so that public bodies subjugate them to an inordinate range of regulations and rules, and to direct intervention into their administration and management. As argued here, the poor record of cooperatives may be due not so much to the social organization of local communities as to a more fundamental inability of the national superstructure to establish the prerequisites and incentives required for deepened market integration and economic growth.

Thus, to understand the location pattern and behaviour of cooperatives, or any establishments, and their influence on economic and social process in geographical space, it becomes necessary to shift the focus of inquiry towards their interdependencies within a wider set of institutionalized power (cf. Hydén 1973, 1983; Friedman 1973; Gyllström 1977, 1986). In a spatial context, Friedman has defined the concept of power as

"the ability of organizational and institutional actors, located in geographical space, to mobilize and allocate resources in geographical space (manpower, capital and information) and intentionally to structure the decision field of others (i.e. to constrain the decisions of others by policies, rules and commands). ...Both kinds of power (governmental and private economic), I will assume, have the capacity to influence the location decisions of firms and households, the quantity, location and application of resources and the flow of innovations." *(1973:12).*

The origin of the authority held by the state apparatus is of course political. Its execution is encapsulated in a network of institutions and organizations at local, regional and national levels which are sanctioned to prescribe, directly or indirectly, the behaviour of social actors. Although, in a spatial sense, many of these mechanisms can be conceived of as 'invisible' in character they evidently have geographical consequences. With regard to cooperatives, identification and analysis of the nature of this matrix of prescribed, implicitly spatial, interdependencies are necessary to be able to judge its effects on these organizations in terms of their structure, operations, behaviour, performance and local impact.

Research on cooperatives in Africa has been dominated by case studies, partly reflecting the dominance of the 'cooperative vs. community' perspective. In line with the arguments above, the papers presented here pay attention to policies and how prescribed organizational behaviour and interdependencies condition the local consequences of cooperatives.

The military government, which replaced Haile Selassie in 1975, and its ideological wing, the Workers Party of Ethiopia (WPE), favour collective solutions in agricultural development. Service and producer cooperatives are the major agricultural institutions set up by the authorities in order to increase peasant production and transform it along socialist lines. In his paper Ståhl centres analysis around the motives for and character of state intervention in peasant agriculture utilizing these two types of organizations. Social consequences of the actual functioning of cooperatives are explored as well as their degree of effectiveness as a means of appropriating surplus from agriculture and of achieving sustained growth of production.

Already in 1908, the first agricultural cooperative was established in Egypt. In his contribution, Holmén reviews the development strategies which since have been pursued by both the British colonial power and the Egyptian government, and the varying roles these shifting strategies have accorded to cooperatives. The main portion of his analysis explores, on the one hand, relations between political forces, agricultural development policies and the size and structure of the government bodies linked to the cooperative sector and, on the other, the combined impact of this superstructure on the growth, organization and performance of agricultural cooperatives.

In Kenya, private ownership has been the favoured mode of production both in agriculture and industry. Increasingly, however, a development policy with an industrial/urban bias has been accompanied by widening state powers. In agriculture it has involved extended state control over the sphere of circulation, including marketing and services, and thus also agricultural cooperatives. Gyllström's paper explores the development of increased state intervention in the cooperative sector and its effects on organizational structure and geographical distribution of agricultural service societies. The paper also examines how the symbiosis established between the government bureaucracy and cooperative bodies has affected the operational behaviour of primary and

4

secondary societies and its compatibility with the structure and production capacity of smallholder agriculture.

To put the studies on Africa in a somewhat wider perspective, the paper by Hatti and Rundquist refers to agricultural service cooperatives in India. As in Africa, the government has assigned cooperatives an important role in rural and agricultural development policies, particularly with reference to poor strata of the rural population. The focus of the paper is on the relationship between the organizational structure of cooperatives and their local impact, with the latter aspect referring to the ability of cooperatives to improve the social and economic conditions of the rural poor.

LITERATURE

Friedman, J. (1973) 'The Spatial Organization of Power in the Development of Urban Systems'. *Economic Development and Cultural Change*, vol.IV, No.3, pp. 12-50.

Gyllström, B. (1977) *The Organization of Production as a Space-Modelling Mechanism in Underdeveloped Countries*. The Case of Tea Production in Kenya. CWK Gleerup, Lund.

Gyllström, B. (1985) 'Fattigdom och förtryck. Om jordbrukskooperationens utvecklingsbetingelser in Afrika.' *Svensk Geografisk Årsbok Nr. 62*, Lund, pp. 45-62.

Gyllström, B. (1986) *Government vs. Agricultural Marketing Cooperatives in Kenya*. Some Observations on Modes and Consequences of State Intervention. Paper presented at the seminar 'Co-operatives Revisited'. The Scandinavian Institute of African Studies, Uppsala.

Haque, F. (1987) 'Can Small be Bountiful? The Challenge of Africa', pp. 16-20 in *Ceres*, No. 116, vol.29, no.2.

Hydén, G. (1973) *Efficiency versus Distribution in East African Cooperatives*. A Study in Organizational Conflicts. East African Literature Bureau, Nairobi.

Hydén, G. (1983) *No Shortcuts to Progress. African Development Management in Perspective*. Heinemann, London.

Worsley, P. (1971) (ed.) *Two Blades of Grass. Rural Cooperatives in Agricultural Modernization*. Manchester University Press.

CHAPTER 1

ADMINISTERED INTERDEPENDENCES VS SPATIAL INTEGRATION
- The Case of Agricultural Service Cooperatives in Kenya

by Björn Gyllström

In the present paper, attention is focussed on direct and indirect influences of policies and government intervention on the structure, behaviour and impact of agricultural service societies. The empirical material refers to Kenya and constitutes part of a research project carried out during the period 1983-88.[1]

CONCEPTUAL FRAMEWORK

Most smallholders in Sub-Saharan Africa have established exchange relations which at least to some extent link them to a wider economic context. Still, the households meet a main share of their material needs without being directly dependent on horizontal linkages, i.e. interaction with markets. When it occurs, small scale of production and high distance friction usually limits exchange transactions to the immediate umland. This kind of predominantly vertically linked agricultural economy, can be characterized as institutionally fragmented. It operates at a generally low level of technological development and surplus production is limited. The individual production units tend to replicate each other in terms of output mix. When differentiation occurs, it is mainly due to ecological variations.

Under these conditions, rural communities have restricted capacity to indigenously achieve an accelerated and significantly improved utilization of available human and physical resources. To achieve this, a closer integration of smallholder agriculture with the national economy can be seen as a prerequisite. It thus has to involve intensified interaction between smallholder agriculture and other sectors of the economy both through exchange of goods and services and through technology transfers which support specialization, diversification and raised levels of productivity. In this setting, the design, composition and timing of policy measures aimed at realizing a more gainful resource utilization obviously are of decisive importance for the pace and

1. A number of publications and papers dealing with anthropological and sociological aspects have been prepared by H. Hedlund (1986), B. Svensson (1986), Å. Hedenmalm (1985) and M. Samuelsson (1987).

pattern of subsequent social and economic changes. As one such instrument, agricultural service cooperatives have attracted considerable attention among policy makers, not least in eastern and southern Africa. In Kenya, the government has used them extensively for providing first-stage marketing of agricultural produce and, increasingly, for channeling credit services and input supplies to smallholders.

Individual economic self-interest is a decisive cross-cultural force in social reproduction processes (Bates, 1981). Accordingly, the contributions of cooperatives to agricultural and rural development can be expected to be basically determined by their ability to offer smallholders incentives for market integration, i.e. their performance in terms of efficiency and service quality. Factors of central concern to smallholders/members would then include their societies' ability to realize advantageous producer prices and low marketing costs, to offer favourable input prices, to provide credit/loans on attractive terms and, generally, to ensure accessibility, timeliness and reliability of services provided. Hence, a basic requirement to be met by cooperatives would be that producer achievements are returned as rewards superior to those available when smallholders rely on traditional technologies and social institutions.

Conventionally, the local social structure, and in particular its parochial components, are seen as the major determinant of the performance characteristics of cooperatives (Hydén 1983; Widstrand 1972; Worsley 1971). This in turn would be due to the mode of organization cooperatives represent, particularly its democratic features. However, democratic qualities have certainly not been a pertinent characteristic of cooperatives in Kenya. On the contrary, they have been subjugated to an inordinate range of regulations and direct government interventions (Gyllström 1986). Therefore, as seen here, the influence of traditional forces may rather be consequences of an already proven inability of cooperatives to offer appropriate incentives. Profound, but generally neglected determinants of such deficiencies are (i) the 'modern' institutional structure and interdependencies of which cooperatives constitute part, and (ii) the physical/technical characteristics of the local environment facing societies and their members.

As regards the former aspect, the institutional set-up reflects development policies based on a considerable degree of state control of agricultural markets. In Kenya, agricultural policies have entailed promotion of what has been perceived as the economically and/or politically essential segments of the smallholder sector. Within this context cooperatives have been assigned specific roles. Further, to ensure results that comply with intentions, the state has involved itself extensively in their promotion and supervision. This government involvement can be expected to have conditioned the behaviour of individual societies and unions, and, hence, their expansion, performance and impact characteristics.

The second aspect refers to the physical/technical characteristics of the rural environment in which societies operate. These include conditions such as agro-ecology, access to arable land, level of development of transports, communications and social infrastructure, and the degree of economic differentiation. Evidently, these are of consequence for production and transaction costs of both farmers and societies. Further, variations in these respects are of direct consequence for the impact of institutional reforms.

APPROACH AND DATA

Conditioning influences of institutions and environment are examined with respect to four basic characteristics of agricultural service cooperatives, namely their spread, survival, performance and impact characteristics. Spread here refers to registration of societies with respect to rate, activity orientation and geographical location in the periods 1946-62, 1963-1970 and 1971-83. Survival denotes the extent to which societies have managed to maintain at least some kind of activity in each of these periods. Analyses of performance focus on produce sales, payment rates and service quality. As regards the former two types of indicators the data are largely confined to 1982/83. The impact analysis attempts to illuminate basic influences of cooperatives on production and income generation in smallholder agriculture.

The data on which the empirical findings are based were collected in the period 1983-86. A major task has been to identify all individual societies registered since 1946, including those that no longer were active, and to collect and compile information on each society with regard to year of registration, geographical location, activity orientation and year of liquidation (when applicable). This material has been supplemented with information regarding physical-technical characteristics of the operational environment at the 'local' (district) level. For societies that were still active in 1983, additional and more detailed information was collected regarding membership, activities, administration/management, produce sales and payment rates. As regards unions, annual accounts and other internal documentation have constituted the major sources of information.

In addition to these general surveys, in-depth studies were done of 25 societies and unions in four districts, including interviews of management committees and union managers. Three of these societies were also covered by anthropological studies (Hedlund 1986).

At the central level, documentation at the Ministry of Co-operative Development constituted the main sources of information pertaining both to

MOCD itself, to the activities of donor agencies and to the structure, staff and operations of cooperative organizations at the national level.

SPREAD

In 1896, the Imperial British East Africa Company commenced construction of a railway intended to give Uganda access to the Indian Ocean (the port at Mombasa). The railway reached Lake Victoria in 1901. In Kenya, it became an influential factor in triggering white settlement on ca. three million hectares of high-altitude land (Leys, 1975).

Two land ordinances, enacted by the colonial administration in 1902 and 1915, provided for the alienation of land and the terms under which land could be acquired by settlers. Some land was unoccupied or sparsely populated. In other cases land was alienated under the pretext that buffer zones had to be established between hostile tribes. Over 80 per cent of the African population were confined to the Native Reserves (Figure 2). A majority lived in two large clusters of reserves along the eastern and western boarders of the Highlands, in the Kikuyu (Central Province) and Kavirondo (S. Nyanza and Western Provinces) areas (Soja 1968).

About half of the European area was arable land of which the largest proportion was mixed farmland yielding a wide variety of crops, and also was suited for keeping dairy cattle. Although important in terms of total output, ranches and coffee/tea plantations supported comparatively few Europeans. Instead it was the large-scale mixed farms which formed the economic base for the majority of settlers, and which also constituted the political nexus of the colony (Leo 1984).

With the development of large-scale agriculture in the White Highlands followed investments in infrastructure, communications and administration. Distant farming areas were connected by branch lines to the main railway and, as a consequence, interior nodes increased in size and importance. The railways and subsequent investments in the road network and public and commercial services established the general urban pattern of Kenya. By 1914, about 2400 km of motorable roads had been built, primarily to serve growing settler areas. The 1920s were characterized by intensive road construction and already then, the settler economy was linked to fairly sophisticated systems of transportation, communication and administration which also supported urban centres providing the settler economy with commercial services. Telephone and postal services also developed rapidly. By 1945, almost all major telephone exchanges were still located in the White Highlands. Postal services showed a similar pattern, having spread outwards from the railway with the growth of European settlement and having a poor service network in the reserves (Soja 1968).

This core of transmission and control facilities were necessary for the build-up, and subsequent maintenance, of large scale western production technologies. At the same time, however, it is apparent that this economy could not have survived had it not, by means of repression and exploitation, been subsidized by a large segment of the colony's African population. A range of policies were applied by the colonial government to assure this system of privilege (Kitching 1980; Leys 1975, van Zwanenberg 1975).

By the end of World War II, distinct regional differences had emerged. Apart from the profound duality caused by the way European areas had been built up, there was, as earlier indicated, also considerable differences among African areas. Ecologically favoured and densely populated areas, in close proximity to the White Highlands, had been penetrated not only by the administration but were also linked to markets for labour, goods and services based on exchange transactions in money. Commercialization of agriculture had begun in the twenties and then focussed on cereals, mainly maize, and during the thirties were added cotton, wattle and vegetables. The subsequent expansion of the monetized economy favoured mainly the highland districts, particularly in the central parts of Kenya.

With very few exceptions, African farmers were not permitted to grow the more profitable cash crops such as coffee, tea and pyrethrum. The exceptions were a small number of farmers in Kisii, Embu and Meru, who had been granted coffee licenses in 1933. This was done on a trial basis within a programme for agricultural production initiated by the colonial administration in 1930 (Kitching 1980). During the latter half of the 1940s, the colonial authorities more seriously began to encourage the expansion of African cash cropping. The main reason was deteriorating living conditions in the reserves, not least in what today is Central Province. These changes were reflected in the introduction of a plan for land rehabilitation. Over a ten year period, starting in 1946, about K.Shs 120 million was to be spent for prevention of soil erosion (Leo 1984).

The same year a Department of Co-operative Development was established. A new Cooperative Act (1945) was promulgated, replacing the Act of 1931, with the explicit aim of fostering marketing co-operatives among the African population (Ouma 1980). The Department was charged with the responsibility of promoting and controlling societies and of educating the members and the public on the usefulness of co-operative efforts, with emphasis on rural areas. Initially, the staff was composed of the Registrar, four inspectors and two clerks (Ouma 1980). During the first few years, the response was predominantly negative, in some cases even hostile (Karanja 1974). Most African businessmen

Figure 1: Administrative Districts, 1983

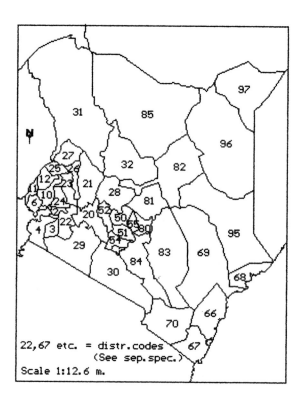

2	KISUMU	23	U.GISHU	50	NYERI	80	EMBU
3	KISII	24	NANDI	51	MURANGA	81	MERU
4	S.NYANZA	25	T-NZOIA	52	NYANDARUA	82	ISIOLO
6	SIAYA	26	E.MARAKWET	54	KIAMBU	83	KITUI
10	KAKAMEGA	27	WEST POKOT	55	KIRINYAGA	84	MACHAKOS
11	BUNGOMA	28	LAIKIPIA	66	KILIFI	85	MARSABIT
12	BUSIA	29	NAROK	67	KWALE	95	GARISSA
20	NAKURU	30	KAJIADO	68	LAMU	96	WAJIR
21	BARINGO	31	TURKANA	69	TANA RIVER	97	MANDERA
22	KERICHO	32	SAMBURU	70	TAITA TAVETA		

Figure 2: Alienated areas and major rural population concentrations in 1962.

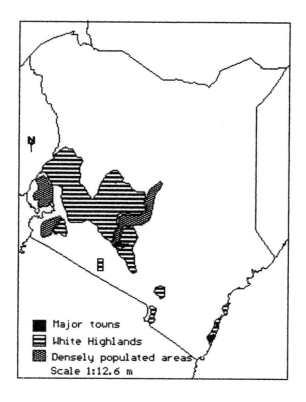

being informed about the object and organization of co-operative societies saw them either as some kind of inferior 'herding' arrangement invented by the administration, or as a potential threat to their own position in the local economy. As these entrepreneurs usually constituted an influential segment of the elite at the local level, their defiance of co-operatives effectively hampered their acceptance by smallholders in general (Hydén 1973). As could be expected, these difficulties were particularly pronounced in Central Province with its commercially more advanced economy (Figure 3a).

In the 1950s, agricultural service cooperatives were increasingly used as an organizational means of influencing and controlling, politically and economically strategic strata of the smallholder community. This was clearly the case under the Swynnerton plan, launched in 1954 largely in response to growing political unrest in rural areas. According to the plan, which focussed on Central and Eastern provinces, all high-quality land would be surveyed and enclosed. So called progressive farmers were to be given access to credit and extension services, and be allowed to grow earlier prohibited cash crops like coffee and pyrethrum. All marketing of these and several other principal cash crops were organized on a cooperative basis. Thus, for a farmer to obtain a license for cultivation of coffee, he had to be member of a primary society. These requirements in basic respects determined the pattern of society registrations in the period 1955-62. The typical feature of the spread pattern is that it reflected the ability of the more commercialized, affluent and/or loyal sectors of the farming population to grasp economic opportunities offered by the administration (Figure 3b).

A third wave of registrations followed with the introduction and expansion of settlement schemes in Rift Valley province. An overriding objective, at least during the first years of independence, was to create political stability in rural areas. In this regard the land issue was of critical importance, and particularly the land in the former White Highlands. This is clearly reflected in the activity orientation of societies registered during the first years of independence. Almost 2/3 of the total number of new societies were either farm purchase or settlement societies. The remainder of registrations, approx. 200, were concentrated to the central highlands and, in terms of activity orientation, to coffee, pyrethrum and dairy (Figure 3c).

The imprint of state powers was magnified after 1966 when a new Co-operative Societies Act was promulgated. To improve the effectiveness of government support and control, their operations were increasingly integrated with a national superstructure of organizations which apart from MOCD has come to comprise of the CBK, KNFC, Cooperative College and CIS.[2] It was no doubt hoped that, taken together, these measures would stimulate economic growth, stem opposition among the upper strata of the farmer community, and thus also facilitate improved political control (Lamb 1974).

In the 1970s, in response to decelerating economic growth and increasing social and regional inequalities, economic and rural development policies were adjusted (ILO 1972). Within this context, the role of cooperatives was redefined and widened. Increasing emphasis now was laid on their role as a delivery system for channeling production credit and inputs to smallholder agriculture, with the intention of contributing to the spread of more input intensive technologies and revitalization of the agricultural economy. The reorientation was combined with increased financial and technical development support to cooperatives in lagging or agriculturally less favoured regions. This is clearly reflected in the geographical distribution of major, donor supported, development programmes, initiated in the 1970s (Figures 3e, f and 4).

Basically, the approach was used as a substitute for rather than supplement to other measures that could create sustained improvements of employment and income opportunities, such as land redistribution, expanded investment in rural infrastructure and liberalization of the economy. It therefore just added to earlier state initiatives aimed at 'capturing the peasantry' (Hydén 1983).

In summary, available data on the expansion pattern characterizing the cooperative sector during the period 1946-83 support the following general observations.

Activity orientation. A decisive factor conditioning the registrations of societies has been government regulations stipulating that smallholders - below a specified size of the holding - had to be members of cooperative societies in order to have access to market channels for certain types of produce. This has applied to coffee, pyrethrum, sugar, cotton (though not since the early 1980s) and, to a certain extent, dairy. The adoption of any of these activities thus had to be preceded by the registration of a primary cooperative society.

A second type of registration regulated by the state has been that of settlement societies. In this case, however, the main concern behind the ordinance was not so much promotion of commercialized agriculture as orderly repayment of settler loans. In addition to these regulation-induced registrations of societies, there has also been the more genuine cases. Judging from available data, though, these constitute a small share of the total number of registrations.

---

2. CBK: Co-operative Bank of Kenya. KNFC: Kenya National Federation of Co-operatives. CIS: Co-operative Insurance Society.

Phasing. Periods with high frequencies of registration are all characterized by specific government initiatives. These were the late 40s, the second half of the 50s, the mid-60s and the late 70s. The first peak was largely a result of campaigns carried out by the Registrar of Co-operatives in areas west of Rift Valley. A second wave of registrations resulted from the implementation of the Swynnerton Plan, a third from the government's settlement programme, and the latest from the introduction of input intensive technologies and a reorientation of development support towards smallholder areas with low income levels and/or stagnating agriculture. In this context, it is interesting to note that variations in registration frequency do not in any systematic manner follow the growth performance of the agricultural economy.

A variety of means have been used for inducing or persuading smallholders to join societies, including campaigns, crop-specific conditions, loan regulations (settlement), and access to credit and farm inputs. The considerable effectiveness of these measures, in terms of generating society registrations, imply responsiveness among smallholders to opportunities perceived to contribute to improved material conditions. Hence, the manner in which cooperatives have been promoted is likely to have effectively cultivated the view among smallholders that the major quality of cooperatives has been their access to resources provided by the state. Under the circumstances, the widespread perception among members of the vertical relation state-cooperative-member as the critical one is fully understandable. Evidently, however, this kind of rationale runs counter to the kind of logic conventionally expected to govern the formation of cooperatives.

Geographical distribution. The ecological limits for the types of produce dependent on cooperative marketing have determined the basic geographical pattern of registrations. Changes in spread profile over time thus is a function of this factor in combination with specific government initiatives. Before independence, registrations were concentrated to campaign areas and to the major coffee zones east and west of Rift Valley. In the sixties, the pattern became more dispersed, reflecting both the implementation of settlement programmes and the 'cooperativization' of the cotton industry in the Lake Victoria region. At the same time, registration densities were increasing in all major smallholder areas. After the mid-70s, the pattern became even more dispersed, now reflecting active state support directed towards economically lagging smallholder areas, including ecologically more marginal lands (Figure 3).

SURVIVAL

In the period 1946-83, the survival rate of societies was continuously rising, from 41 per cent in 1946-62 to 67 per cent in 1963-70, and 72 per cent in 1971-83. Prior to 1971 a clear relation could be observed between survival rates and regional variations in 'operational environment'. The latter concept denotes variations in conditions that influence the prospects of commercial agricultural production. These include ecology, land tenure, density of transport network, levels of education, population density, and degree of economic differentiation. Thus, in environments favoured in terms of agro-ecology and infrastructure, cooperatives generally displayed lower mortality rates. Survival was also influenced by the kind of produce handled by the societies. Cooperatives which enjoyed a local marketing monopoly for specific types of produce thus generally displayed higher survival rates (Table 1, Figure 5a, 6a).

Table 1: Survival rates by categories of activity and local environment, 1963-70[1]. Excluding secondary societies (unions).

Environm	Coffee No. in reg Surv(%)		Other Pre- ferential Produce No. in reg Surv(%)		Other Produce No. in reg Surv(%)		Total No. in reg Surv(%)	
C1 63/70	101	88	117	78	243	60	461	71
C2 63/70	42	88	63	70	44	35	149	64
C3 63/70	17	100	41	75	132	51	190	61
C4 63/70	2	50	9	12	58	31	69	29
Total/ Aver %	162	89	230	73	477	51	869	64

1) Districts taxonomized according to agro-ecology, proportion of adjudicated land, population density, road density, proportion of children in school, and level of economic differentiation. C1 represents districts/environments that according to this taxonomy offer the most favourable conditions. See Gyllström 1988, Ch.3.

Source: Survey data.

Figure 3a: Registrations of Agricultural Service Societies, 1946-53.

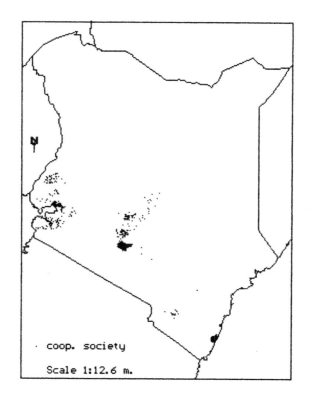

coop. society

Scale 1:12.6 m.

Source: Survey Data

17

Figure 3b: Registrations of Agricultural Service Societies, 1954-62.

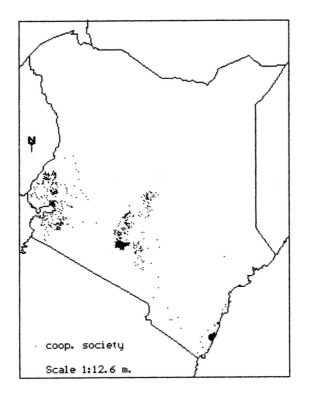

Source: Survey Data

Figure 3c: Registrations of Agricultural Service Societies, 1963-66

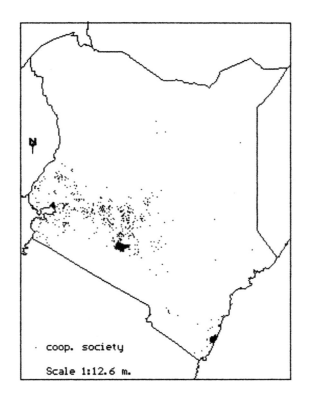

coop. society

Scale 1:12.6 m.

Source: Survey Data

19

Figure 3d: Registrations of Agricultural Service Societies, 1967-72.

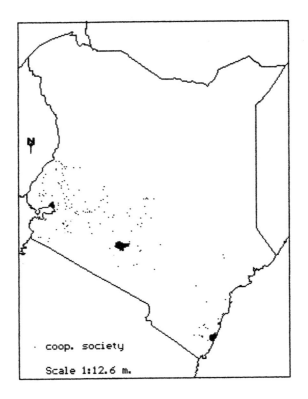

Source: Survey Data

20

Figure 3e: Registrations of Agricultural Service Societies, 1973-77.

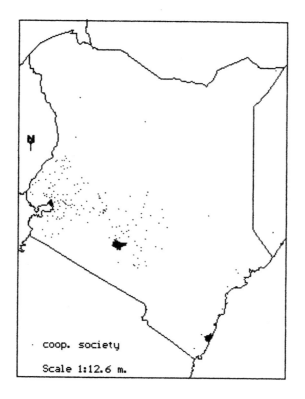

coop. society

Scale 1:12.6 m.

Source: Survey Data

Figure 3f: Registrations of Agricultural Service Societies, 1978-83.

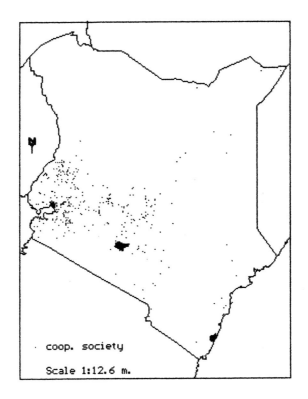

coop. society

Scale 1:12.6 m.

Source: Survey Data

Figure 4a: Integrated Agricultural Development Project I

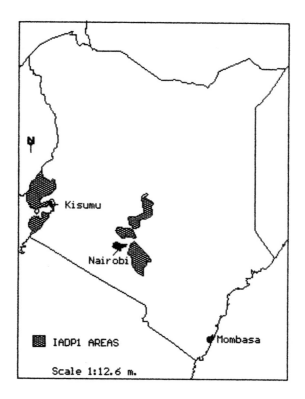

Source: Research and Evaluation Unit, MOCD, 1981

Figure 4b: Integrated Agricultural Development Project II

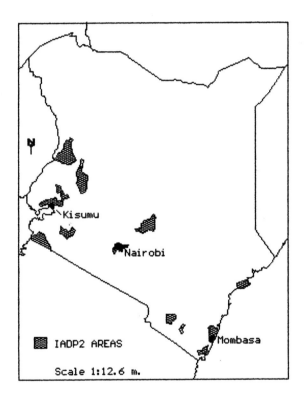

Source: Research and Evaluation Unit, MOCD, 1981

Figure 4c: Smallholder Production Services and Credit Programme

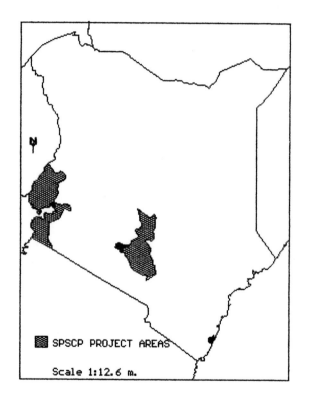

Source: Research and Evaluation Unit, MOCD, 1981

<u>Figure 4d</u>: Farm Input Supply Scheme

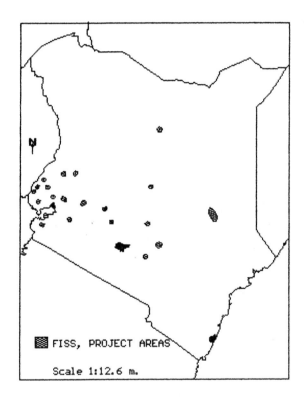

Source: Research and Evaluation Unit, MOCD, 1981

Figure 4e: Smallholder Coffee Improvement Project

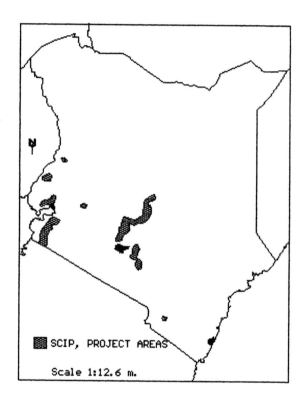

Source: Research and Evaluation Unit, MOCD, 1981

Figure 4f: Machakos Integrated Development Programme

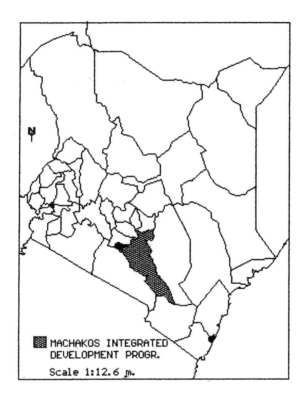

Source: Research and Evaluation Unit, MOCD, 1981

Figure 4g: Kitui Arid and Semi-Arid Lands Project

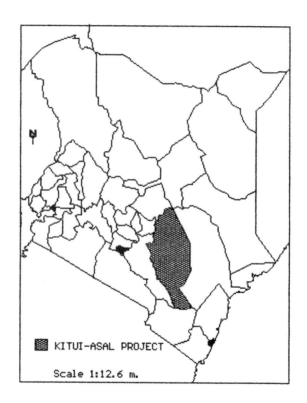

Source: Research and Evaluation Unit, MOCD, 1981

Figure 5a: Categories of Environments, 1963-70.

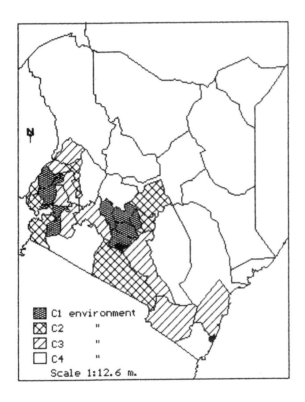

Source: Population Census 1969,1979. Statistical Abstr., Various Issues 1963-83
Ministry of Co-operative Development, District Annual Reports. Survey Data

Figure 5b: Categories of Environments, 1971-83.

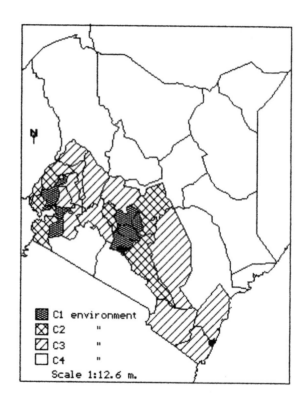

Source: Population Census 1969,1979. Statistical Abstr., Various Issues 1963-83
Ministry of Co-operative Development, District Annual Reports. Survey Data

Figure 6a: Liquidated/Dormant Agricultural Service Societies, 1963-70

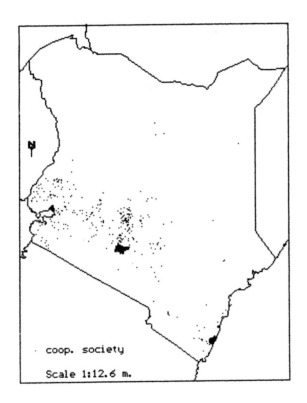

coop. society

Scale 1:12.6 m.

Source: Survey Data.

32

Figure 6b: Liquidated/Dormant Agricultural Service Societies, 1971-83.

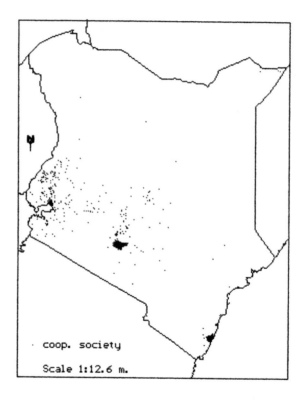

Source: Survey Data.

Table 2: Survival rates by categories of activity and local environment, 1971-83 Excluding secondary societies (unions).

Environment	Coffee No. in reg Surv(%)		Other Preferential Produce No. in reg Surv(%)		Other Produce No. in reg Surv(%)		Total No.in reg Surv(%)	
C1 71/83	78	94	124	88	120	35	322	69
C2 71/83	87	95	81	77	203	66	371	75
C3 71/83	4	75	48	94	179	68	231	73
C4 71/83	1	100	3	66	41	52	45	53
TOT/AVER %	170	94	256	85	543	58	969	72

Source: Survey data.

In the period 1971-83, the relation environment-survival was less significant, i.e. survival rates were generally high even in more unfavorable environments (Table 2, Figures 5b, 6b). This does not necessarily mean that cooperatives had strengthened their position as marketing and supply organizations. As a matter of fact, aggregate indicators show that while the survival ability of primary societies improved, their performance, in terms of value of marketed production, deteriorated. Thus, in the period 1971-83, their combined share of smallholders' value of gross marketed production fell from 48 to 43 per cent.

The fact that this contraction took place in a context where the agricultural sector as a whole suffered from decelerating growth, underlines their generally poor performance.

PERFORMANCE

To understand the reasons behind improved survival on the one hand and deteriorating performance on the other, it is necessary to consider the organizational structure that has evolved in the cooperative sector. The Cooperative Societies Act of 1966 considerably strengthened state control of cooperatives. Promulgation of the new legislation was probably assisted by the crisis then facing cooperatives. Thus, following the large number of registrations in the early 1960s, there was a felt need to stem a wave of reported cases of mismanagement and misappropriations (Hydén 1973). More important, however, was probably the perception that cooperatives could be developed into a feasible instrument for integrating smallholders with the modern economy. In this role they would offer a service network in rural areas which combined first-stage processing and marketing with supply of credit and inputs. Realization of these aspirations required a rational and orderly development of the cooperative sector. Given the perceived lack of adequate knowledge and organizational capacity in rural areas, it was therefore seen as axiomatic that the government would have to be the modus operandi in designing and directing this process. Hence, an acceptable level of effectiveness could be ensured only with the support of the power, resources and organization of the state.

At the policy level, it was made clear that the government defined the basic activity pattern. Co-operatives would have to accept to operate within a prescribed range of marketing activities:

"Since Independence, the Government has set up a number of state trading corporations, agricultural marketing boards and has encouraged the development of companies partly or wholly owned by Africans.. . Within this policy the co-operative movement will be expected to improve its performance and to compete unhindered "... *in those spheres of the economy in which it is allowed to participate."* (my emphasis) (Republic of Kenya 1970:2).

In practice this meant that the marketing activities of societies were oriented towards a range of specified types of produce, typically of high-value, export and non-food character. As each of the types of produce given priority[3] have different ecological requirements (except dairy vs. coffee and pyrethrum), these geared the marketing activities of each individual society towards one specific product. This mono-marketing structure was to be further reinforced by the administrative blueprint the government imposed on societies (see below). The government also established a basic three-tiered organizational structure of the cooperative sector consisting of a federation at the national level (KNFC), secondary societies (unions) and primary societies. Geographically, each union would cover a district with existing primary societies as members.

In achieving technological development and accelerated growth in agriculture, lack of credit was seen as a binding constraint. The main commercial activity to be developed within the cooperative sector, alongside marketing services, was therefore the supply of credit and inputs. Through the establishment of the Co-operative Bank of Kenya (CBK) a platform was created for pooling and attracting financial resources for on-lending to the cooperative sector.

---

3. Coffee, pyrethrum, cotton, sugar, dairy, cashew.

The basic architecture outlined above was not seen as enough. The real challenge was to ensure that the activities designated for cooperatives were carried out by appropriately organized unions and societies, and at a certain level of management standard. This required first and foremost a technically rational organization of unions and societies. One practical aspect of how to achieve the organizational transformation perceived as necessary, had been cleared with the advent of the new cooperative legislation. It granted the government almost unlimited rights to interfere in and regulate the administration and management of individual societies and unions.

To realize this, however, required technical knowledge which at the time was critically short in supply in societies and unions, and, not least, in the government bureaucracy. External technical assistance became the remedy. This was not seen as a negative feature; if anything it was expected to ensure the design of efficient administration and management systems. In the late 60s and most of the 70s, during which period the organizational development can be seen as having been of decisive importance, expatriate staff played an important role. One indication of the critical shortage of certain Kenyan key staff that prevailed is that the 'accounts development and implementation' function of the Department of Co-operative Development was exclusively staffed by expatriate personnel.

Although the donor agencies contributed with a considerable number of technical staff, the total staff requirements increased dramatically both in the cooperatives and the 'superstructure' (Table 3). This inflation of the 'national superstructure' was more a consequence of the institution-building process than of the growth in number of societies, membership and sales. This becomes evident when examining some pertinent features of the introduced organizational and administrative architecture. These changes were seen as essential both for effectively achieving *functional* and *institutional* integration of the cooperative sector.

As regards functional integration, it focussed on devising administrative systems for linking the primary societies' marketing activities with credit and input supply services. It was preceded by revisions of the accounting systems. A first step was the introduction of a standardized accounts plan, followed by routines for budgets, trial balances, cash control, final accounts and the use of loose leaf ledgers. A decisive step in the reformation of the accounts systems was the introduction of produce-specific 'member transaction systems' (MT-system), facilitating administratively integrated recording and control of all transactions, related to marketing, input supplies and payments, between a member and his society.

Table 3: Staff establishment in DOCD/MOCD and central cooperative institutions, 1963-83.[1]

	1963	1973	1983
DOCD/MOCD	163	619	1869
KNFC	10	28	130
CBK	-	16	219
Coop. College	-	28	148
CIS	-	-	43
Total	173	691	2409

1) DOCD; Department of Co-operative Development. MOCD; Ministry of Co-operative Development. KNFC; Kenya National Federation of Co-operatives. CBK; Co-operative Bank of Kenya. CIS; Co-operative Insurance Society.

Source: Internal documentation at MOCD, KNFC, CBK, and CIS.

The institutional aspect concerned two principal issues, (i) the integration of primary societies with unions at the district level, and (ii) devising procedures and systems facilitating effective government supervision and development support.

As regards the first aspect, the structure of the accounting system was the prime device for administrative integration of primary societies with the unions. Thus, primary societies were assigned only the physical operations and the basic recording of members' transactions. Such accounting tasks as posting of documents, ledger postings, payment calculations, trial balancing and final accounts were centralized to the unions. Further, in order to "achieve greater efficiency faster" (Republic of Kenya 1970), primary societies would have to accept all services offered by the unions. The range of such services varies among unions depending on their size and differentiation but usually includes, apart from centralized accounting, procurement of inputs, and credit and transport services. As regards the input supplies, unions would bulk orders from primary societies, organize the actual purchases of farm inputs and distribute the goods to the society stores. In addition the unions might have their own stores for resale. The credit sections established in the unions for administration of production credit were in some cases extended into banking sections. In the latter case, members of primary societies could open their own savings account which then also would be credited any proceeds from produce sales.

This reorganization was the result of direct government intervention and was made possible by the Co-operative Societies Act of 1966 and the Co-operative Societies Rules of 1969. The legislation gave the government wide powers of control, and through the organizational transformation implemented in the 60s and 70s, supervisory elements were built into the administration and management of cooperatives. Routines were established that ensured that the operations of cooperatives were proceeding according to a 'stop-and-check' system. Thus hardly any kind of activity could be carried out without being subjected either to direct approval or control by government officers.

This was facilitated by the 'systems approach' followed in the transformation of societies and unions. Intra- and inter- organizational activities were defined and formalized (documented) as sequenced procedures (routines), thereby prescribing the 'standard behaviour' of the staff of societies and unions. This 'command style' of organizational design obviously facilitates close government control. Thus, this aspect rather than more independent modes of management was assigned prime significance. As a result, we can talk about a cooperative sector with practically all actors being subjected to detailed regulation. At local, regional and national levels the division of activities created a cobweb of prescribed interdependencies among societies, unions, central bodies and the administrative hierarchy of the ministry. In basic respects, the strategy reflects a populist-oriented philosophy which incorporates a central position for the state in the national economy both in relation to overall planning (regulation) and direct intervention, resulting in extended control over the sphere of circulation (marketing, banking, services) and, to some extent, production (cf. Ilchman and Bhargava 1973).

If accepting that the symbiosis with government institutions may have favourably influenced the survival capacity of cooperatives, it has at the same time negatively affected both their commercial performance and their possible contributions to agricultural and rural development. In a technical sense, the entire construct may seem internally coherent. However, it displays fundamental weaknesses when exposed to the vagaries of the environment on which it essentially depends, i.e. the smallholder economy. It then becomes evident that the design rests on a number of implicit assumptions that may be met only in industrially organized environments, such as ease of interaction in geographical space, a certain scale of operation, management skills and stability. These threshold requirements, imparted on societies and unions, can in most cases be met only partly, if at all. This has in fundamental respects conditioned the expected rationality and benefits of cooperatives.

Installed scale and interaction

The administrative integration of payments for produce deliveries and the provision of credit/inputs through a recording and accounting system is costly. First, independently of the actual scale of operation, there is the cost of maintaining the system, i.e. to pay for qualified staff, equipment and stationary. Secondly, practically every transaction between a member and his society results in a number of records. Hence, the share of farmers' gross payments deducted to cover the society's operations will be dependent not only on total turnover but also on the number and average value of transactions between members and the society.

The organizational construct 'single-produce/multipurpose', and the administrative systems on which it depends, are imposing threshold requirements that in most cases cannot be met by the rural environments in which the societies operate. The type of output marketed by a society is usually produced by only a portion of smallholders within its area of operation. To satisfy scale requirements set by the society's fixed overhead costs ('threshold size'[4]), it will have to cover a relatively large umland. Also, low productivity at the farm level, due to agro-ecology, poor infrastructure and other reasons, contributes to push the boundaries of the area of operation outwards. At the same time distance friction is high. Hence, with increasing size of the area of operation, transport costs will escalate and the service quality (farmers' access to services) deteriorate.

Thus, there is a basic incompatibility between organizations with sizeable, built-in scale requirements and rural environments with unstable production, low agricultural productivity and high costs of interaction. The latter types of deterrents, in turn, may be the singular or combined result of factors such as unfavorable agro-ecological conditions, land fragmentation, inadequate transport networks and poorly developed social and commercial infrastructure. At the aggregate level, tables 5 and 6 support the prevalence of these relations.

---

4. This obviously varies depending on the type of produce a society is marketing. Operationalizing the concept, and disregarding variations caused by differences in management performance, it can be argued that a society is able to operate at an acceptable scale if payments to members exceed 80 per cent of the price paid to the society (gross payment).

Table 4: Value of marketed produce 1982/83, by activity orientation (primary societies). K.Sh. '000.

Activity	Act. no	no of societies	Value of marketed prod	Tot no of members
Cereals	11	38	53,372	10,988
Coffee	12	171	1839,528	506,533
Cotton	13	54	42,449	92,492
Pyrethrum	15	79	28,504	82,981
Sugar cane	17	54	84,654	27,670
Dairy	21	253	291,735	146,560
Misc.		139	90,720	77,224
Total		788	2430,962	944,388

Source: Survey data.

Table 5: Value of marketed produce by type of environment, 1982/83. K.Sh.'000.

Environm	no of districts	no of societies	Value of marketed produce	Average sales/soc	Tot no of members
C1	7	244	1,433,347	5,874	490,536
C2	9	307	825,311	2,679	374,431
C3	10	209	160,133	766	71,151
C4	11	28	12,081	431	8,270
Total	37	788	2,430,962	3,081	944,388

Source: Survey data.

Table 6: Value of marketed produce by type of environment, excl. coffee societies, 1982/83. K.Sh. '000.

Environm	Number of societies	Value of marketed produce	Average sales/soc	Tot no of members
C1	165	225,728	1,368	214,042
C2	223	201,404	903	155,891
C3	205	155,642	771	65,170
C4	26	11,947	460	7,743
Total	619	594,721	961	442,846

Source: Survey data.

Although coffee societies display a performance record that is superior to societies marketing other types of produce, they can be used to exemplify some of our arguments. Coffee is a high value crop in terms of returns per hectare. As cherry is heavy and bulky in relation to 'clean' (parchment) coffee, local first-stage processing is necessary. This is done at society-owned hulling units ('coffee factories') which each covers a very limited geographical area. After hulling and drying, the society delivers the coffee to the agent of the marketing board. The administrative infrastructure and requirements are approximately identical among societies, independently of scale of operation (volume of sales) with obvious consequences for the payment rate to members of small societies. Also the hulling costs are affected by variations in volume. Thus a factory increasing its output from 150 to 240 tonnes of cherry (50%) may cut its unit costs by one-third.

The payment rate to members closely follows value of parchment sales (Table 7). Evidently it also covaries with members' average sales of cherry. It can also be seen that in all but one size interval (<2.0), the pay ratio is higher in the more favourable type of environment (C1). About 1/3 of the total number of members of coffee societies realize a payment rate exceeding 80 per cent. All of them are members of societies with sales exceeding K.Shs 10 million and only a fraction are living outside the C1-environment. Considering more specifically concentration and the geographical location of societies, it can be seen that 46 coffee societies, out of 171, accounted for 77 per cent of total coffee sales and for almost 4/5 of the total payments to farmers. Most of these societies are located within a fairly limited area of Central Province.

Table 7: Basic performance characteristics of primary coffee societies by type
of environment and size category (parchment sales), 1982/83.

Environm Categ.	Size Categ Parchm Sales Mill Shs	no of Societies	Parchm Sales Mill Shs	Member- Ship ('000)	Average Sales/ Member Shs	Pay Ratio %
C1	< 2.0	23	16.5	24.4	680	68.1
	2.0 - 3.9	14	41.6	37.0	1125	73.1
	4.0 - 5.9	8	38.4	26.4	1450	74.3
	6.0 - 9.9	7	58.0	23.7	2440	74.9
	10.0-19.9	5	77.4	13.5	5730	83.8
	20.0-29.9	8	188.5	32.3	5830	84.8
	30.0-49.9	8	299.8	40.7	7360	83.2
	>49.9	7	481.1	76.5	6290	84.3
Subtotal		80	1201.3	274.5	4380	82.7
C2	< 2.0	27	25.5	26.8	950	71.7
	2.0 - 3.9	11	34.5	21.2	1630	71.3
	4.0 - 5.9	7	33.0	22.1	1490	71.3
	6.0 - 9.9	21	165.5	63.1	2620	73.6
	10.0-19.9	9	131.6	36.3	3615	78.9
	20.0-29.9	6	136.0	44.1	3085	77.5
	30.0-49.9	3	104.1	8.1	12870	80.6
Subtotal		84	620.3	222.0	2840	76.4

Source: Survey data, MOCD.

In summary, the performance profile of coffee cooperatives illustrates the
importance of the interrelations between scale economies and environment.
The former are largely a consequence of wholesale implementation of omnibus
and demanding administrative systems. For a society to operate above this
created threshold level requires high farm productivity, a fairly large
membership and low interaction costs. This is also what characterizes the rural
economy of Central Province. In this environment, the kind of cooperative

societies considered here apparently can make a useful contribution in the rural economy. When the opposite is true, which is the most common case, the organizational design locks the individual society in a high-cost trap from which it cannot escape, unless technical, institutional and economic changes significantly raise the production capacity of the smallholder economy. The point is that such changes cannot in any substantial way be triggered or induced by cooperatives. If anything, they are likely to delay such processes by blocking alternative, more efficient commercial operations.

In this context also the development of unions is illustrative. With the rapid expansion of credit and input supply services, starting in the early 1970s, financial and technical support was concentrated to the unions. In the major schemes it resulted in additional investments in storage facilities and stock, offices, vehicles, staff training, and in temporary subsidies to cover the increased costs following from expansion of the unions' administration and staff. The strategy evidently built on very optimistic assumptions regarding the effectiveness of centralized intervention and administratively rationed incentives. Thus, generated business volumes were simply too small in relation to the size and cost of maintaining the organizational superstructure. In essential respects, operations were curtailed by managerial complexity and difficulties in maintaining effective linkages to individual members, primary societies, the cooperative bank and the government bureaucracy.

Thus, frequently loans to members were too large in relation to what would be possible to achieve in terms of increased farm production, and often the loans were dispersed at the wrong time. In other cases, loans were correctly allocated but inputs or transports for their distribution were lacking. These shortcomings no doubt contributed to high frequencies of repayment failures among members. Farmers owing their society money obviously tried to avoid dealing with it. Thus, if member deliveries accelerated at all, the growth was more often than not temporary in nature. In the absence of anticipated effects, administratively and operationally overloaded unions ran into financial and operational difficulties.

By 1983, practically all unions, except those linked to societies marketing coffee, played a marginal role as suppliers of inputs. Ten coffee unions which operated in environments favoured in terms of agro-ecology and infrastructure, then accounted for 85 per cent of total cooperative input sales and for 2/3 of total turnover. Most of the 22 non-coffee unions operated at a loss in 1982/83, and generally their position was precarious. Commonly, they had been unable to accumulate own capital. With a realistic assessment of the unions' assets, it seems clear that almost half of them should have been liquidated. Continued survival has been made possible by ad hoc-like support from the government and donor agencies. Although coffee unions performed better than other

Table 8: Selected performance features of unions, by type of local environment, 1982/83. K.Sh. million.

Environment	no. of unions	Sales of inputs	turnover	Total Result
C1	12	123.2	205.4	10.4
C2	17	45.1	176.9	-6.7
C3	5	8.8	17.3	1.0
C4	1	0.0	0.2	0.1
Total	35	177.1	399.8	4.8

Source: Survey data and union accounts.

unions, their position was not entirely acceptable. In several cases their liquidity position was unsatisfactory, and generally too many activities were operated at a loss (about 45 per cent). The unions also seemed to have a preference for getting involved in activities of limited relevance to affiliated societies and their members.

With reference to primary societies it was earlier argued that their mode of organization results in threshold requirements (if expected to operate at an acceptable level of efficiency) that usually are incompatible with the types of environments in which they do operate. In the case of unions, this consequence is even more pronounced. The 'threshold' issue, following from the imposed mode of organization is however closely related also to another aspect, namely the prescribed management behaviour of societies and unions.

Management systems and interorganizational dependencies

Management is obviously affected already by the complexity of the administrative systems. Further, as the systems are designed and implemented by the government, within the context of its cooperative development policy, they are prescriptions rather than guide-lines. Hence, the government devotes a large staff and considerable other resources to ensure that the mechanics of the different systems are adhered to. At an operational level this means that societies and unions slavishly replicate 'manualized' directives and ad hoc invented rulings, which by the bureaucracy are perceived as both necessary and sufficient to ensure efficient operations.

The nature of this set-up constitutes a severe managerial constraint. Thus, administrative functions and service activities are split between cooperative establishments and government offices in ways which make primary societies, in particular, partial management units. As indicated above, a number of essential functions are centralized to the unions such as book-keeping, credit administration, recruitment and deployment of certain staff categories, transport services, and procurement of inputs. This does not only mean functional division of tasks and procedures, but also their geographical separation. The resulting spatial network thus contains interdependencies that will necessitate efficient transportation and communication services. This, however, is far from common. Rather the typical case is that transports are unreliable, slow and expensive, that telephones networks are overloaded or do not exist, and that postal services are poor. The critical dependence of this construct on the economy's capacity of supporting spatial integration, becomes even more evident when considering that also decision-making powers are geographically fragmented. Vital decision-making is separated from the establishments performing the member-oriented service activities on which the sector is based, i.e. principally the primary societies.

In the case of input supplies, the tight coupling of unions with stores and primary societies illustrates the danger of assuming that administratively prescribed interdependencies will result in integration. Although being one of the causes behind the affliction now facing most unions, integration was no doubt assumed to generate considerable economies of scale. However, it then requires that the different levels are synchronized both at the stage of determining types and quantities of inputs and at the stage of actual distribution. Most unions and their affiliated primary societies did not manage to satisfy these basic logistical requirements. These problems were aggravated - not so unexpectedly - by other constraints such that supplies were not coming forward due to temporary shortages, rationing, etc. which the spatially overstretched and rigid managerial set-up was unable to handle.

Since the 1960s, the right to make decisions has rather consistently been pushed upwards in the cooperative hierarchy. At most, the decision-making powers now remaining at the local level can be termed 'conditional', i.e. practically all decisions falling outside the sphere of narrowly defined routine matters have to be approved by externally posted staff. Thus, at a number of levels of the cooperative and governmental hierarchy, and in different geographical locations, we find staff in charge of segments of managerial processes that have been externalized from the societies. However, under the given circumstances, spatially extended processes for decision-making are unstable, time consuming and expensive. Furthermore, decisions are made by staff with limited knowledge about local conditions. Proposals and 'conditionally made decisions' shuttled through the administrative hierarchy therefore tend to be judged from a policy point of view, where the policy either is so diffuse that it leaves ample room for subjective interpretations or is operationalized to a set of simplistic criteria.

Activities at the local level are permeated by these 'stop-and-check' exercises. For example, a society manager cannot make a payment exceeding K.Sh. 200[5] without the approval of a government officer. As a result the manager is forced to spend considerable amounts of time and money on seeking approvals on often trivial issues. Another example is members' loan applications which are subjected to procedures that allocate a variety of administrative and supervisory roles to staff and committee members at the society and union levels as well to MOCD's district and headquarter staff. Further, if a society or union need to make an investment a documented request has to be channeled through the DCO's office for 'policy screening' and possible approval at the MOCD headquarters. These examples can be multiplied. The point is that most activities at the primary society level do not only have to follow a given format. They are also linked to prescribed external dependencies that slow down and complicate execution and grossly inflate costs.

In summary, the design of Kenya's cooperative development policy and its derivatives in the form of legislation, regulations and organizational constructs, show an amazing disregard of the constraints different types of environments may impose. Administratively top-heavy and conformistic organizations have been engineered based on a 'colonial', paternalistic philosophy focussed on control rather than achievement. As a consequence, societies and unions do not only lack managerial autonomy but have built-in scale and skill requirements that can be met only under very favourable circumstances. According to our judgement, only parts of Central Province presently meet these requirements. Here, a relatively high proportion of smallholders are growing coffee under favourable agro-ecological conditions; the province is close to Nairobi, and the rural economy is supported by a well developed physical, social and commercial infrastructure. In most other areas, the operations of cooperatives are seriously constrained.

IMPACT

Smallholders

To indicate the influence of cooperatives on production and living conditions of smallholders, three concepts have been used, namely (i) reach, (ii) functional participation and (iii) reflective participation. Reach simply denotes the extent

---

5. This amount refers to 1985.

to which a cooperative organization is linked to households within its area of operation. Here we define it as the number of rural households that are active members of service societies. Functional participation indicates the degree to which those reached by societies actually take part in its activities as economic actors. By reflective participation is meant the subordination of society activities to members' conscious reflection and decision-making. Finally, the profile of the cooperative sector in the above respects is linked to source of participation. Of three main categories - spontaneous, induced and coerced - the two latter are predominant in Kenya.

Reach. Estimation of the actual number of active households has to take into account the magnitude of double and multiple memberships as well as the number of members who, although being registered, no longer are active. We then arrive at a total reach of agricultural service societies in the range of 600,000-700,000, i.e. around 1/3 of the estimated total number of smallholder households. This evidently is considerably less than the officially stated membership of approx. 1.2 million. Geographically, the distribution of members is more concentrated than that of the total rural population although this feature became less distinctive in the 1970s and early 80s.

Functional participation. Both in terms of turnover and produce sales, four districts in Central Province and two neighbouring districts in Eastern Province constitute a 'core region'. With less than half of the national membership, they accounted for over 70 per cent of turnover and produce sales in 1982/83. While changes in membership in the period 1970-83 were characterized by geographical dispersal, the economic dominance of this core region increased markedly.

It is clear that relatively few societies were of dominating importance. Ranking all societies by sales, we find that the top 10 per cent (78 societies) accounted for almost 3/4 of total produce payments to members. They represented however only 1/3 of the total membership and an estimated 1/10 of the total number of smallholder households. The average sales per member in these societies, of which practically all are found in the so called core region, was in 1983 about K.Sh. 5,000 as compared to K.Sh. 1,200 in other societies.

This bias to the advantage of privileged strata of smallholders is accentuated further when considering credit and input supply services. In the case of 'special credit programmes' we estimate that they have reached something like 5-7 per cent of the smallholder households. The figure for the Co-operative Production Credit Scheme is in the range of 10-12 per cent, though with large regional variations. In some basic respects sales of inputs reflect the distribution of credit among societies and regions. This does not however necessarily indicate the presence of a straight forward causal relation between credit services and sales of inputs. This applies in particular to western Kenya, but even in the case of CPCS the relation is rather ambiguous (Njonjo et. al. 1985). A more significant and regular use of inputs is largely confined to about 250,000 coffee growers in Central and Eastern provinces.

Reflective participation. Cooperative legislation, combined with incalculable administrative systems, constitute the main institutional means of ensuring that members' ability to control their societies has remained limited. Contrary to officially stated intentions, these rights were further restricted in the 1970s and 80s. Members' and committee members' knowledge about the structure and basic management features of their societies, and their rights and obligations as members, can nonetheless be used to indicate their general capacity to exercise the limited rights still remaining. Available evidence indicates that most committee members do not know essentials about the management of their societies. As regards ordinary members, few are effectively reached by relevant information. Due to this, and a generally low level of education, most members were poorly equipped to exercise their rights and thus influence society operations (Standa and Maranga 1981).

Central level

An induced, and partly coerced, mode of participation has characterized cooperative development in Kenya. One aspect of particular interest therefore is to identify contextual and external influences that have conditioned the ways in which strategies have been formulated and their consequences for the structure and performance of the central bureaucracy. As earlier noted, the number of central bodies as well as their size and complexity have increased considerably (Table 3). The growth of this superstructure seems to have been generated by three principal forces, namely national development policies, cooperative policies and legislation, and cooperative development support. As regards the first of these, the high propensity of state intervention in economically important segments of the agricultural sector, partly through cooperatives, certainly has a political rationale. Thus, promotion of development appears basically to have been perceived as equivalent to advancing industry and the urban sector together with the economically and politically most vital segments of the smallholder sector. A central function of the latter has been to contribute to the foreign exchange earnings required for modernization. This element of the strategy, geared towards the promotion of 'progressive' smallholder strata, resembles the philosophy introduced already by the colonial government in the context of the Swynnerton Plan.

The wide-reaching powers assumed by the government bureaucracy through the new cooperative legislation, would in part ensure that the anticipated agricultural growth pattern was realized. This ambition is reflected in the produce orientation, organization and administrative structure of the societies given priority. In the 1960s the serious stratification mechanisms contained by these policies were concealed by the growth generated by 'structural' changes in smallholder agriculture. These consisted of the introduction of previously prohibited cash crops, the settling of smallholders in formerly alienated areas, and the introduction of hybrid maize.

Since the early 1970s, however, the transformation process has been faltering. Agricultural production and the rural economy has stagnated. Urban growth has been fueled more by bureaucratic proliferation than industrial expansion. In the absence of major forces of growth in secondary and tertiary industries in the private sector, and in order to maintain the political support of an increasingly influential urban population, policies with a bias against rural areas in general and smallholder agriculture in particular have continued. Given a rather weak political base, it has at the same time been necessary to maintain a network of allies in rural areas. One way of doing this has obviously been through a selective distribution of benefits and subsidies, for which purpose also the cooperative infrastructure has played a role.

The principal function of agricultural service cooperatives within the framework of national development policies thus has been to secure high rates of growth of produce being of importance as foreign exchange earners. In addition it has facilitated a selective distribution of subsidies and benefits. Since the mid-70s, the subsidization aspect has grown in prominence as reflected in a widened application of cooperative 'supply-side' approaches. While this increased 'itemization' (cf. Harvey et. al. 1979) has left rather few imprints in terms of increased agricultural production, it has had effects on the number of societies and members and, in particular, on the size and complexity of the central bureaucracy. For the polity, promotion of cooperatives along these lines has had the added advantage of giving an impression of progressive rural development efforts while constituting a cheap substitute both for land reforms and critically needed public investment in infrastructure.

In the process of itemization and bureaucratic proliferation has followed a continued appropriation by central bodies of decision-making functions at the primary society and union levels. The means to directly interfere in operations and management were thus strengthened, and tended towards more coercively flavoured modes of promotion. However, the government's ability to positively influence the performance of cooperatives has remained limited (Gyllström 1986). In the 1980s, this ability was further restricted by the stagnation of the national economy. Eventually it has affected the resources made available to the central bureaucracy. As a consequence, the government's mode of implementing its complex supervisory, controlling and promotional obligations has deteriorated into what can be called 'casual micro regulation'.

The economic and political system built up in Kenya has generated considerable privileges for a predominantly urbanized political, bureaucratic and commercial elite. The maintenance of this system has increasingly had to rely on a patrimonial and politically repressive rule. This kind of setting is typically linked not only to coercion and repression, but also has to rely on personal loyalty and patron-client relations. As is well known this kind of environment tends to bolster corruption and incompetence 'not only' in the bureaucracy but also in activities and organizations dependent on government (Sandbrook 1985). For the cooperative sector, the consequences of this kind of decay have been as unfortunate as they have been obvious.

Donor agencies. Since a few years after independence, donor agencies have played an essential role in the development of the cooperative sector in Kenya. Generally, their influence is seen both in the administrative structure of agricultural cooperatives, in the kind of services offered, and in the promotion of cooperatives in disadvantaged regions. The acceptance of cooperatives as the appropriate object of support is no doubt linked to the democratic and other qualities usually associated with this mode of organization. This ideologically and morally justified trust in cooperatives has, rather uncritically, spilled-over to encompass a faith in most types of organizations that in Kenya, and actually in most African countries, happen to have been assigned the etiquette 'cooperative'.

The fact that cooperatives in Kenya have very little in common with conventional service societies thus seems to have been of little concern. Actually, donor agencies' promotion of cooperatives in Kenya has built on an excessively paternalistic philosophy which runs counter to the very meaning of cooperative development. Possibly, the legitimacy assumed to follow from channeling support through the state machinery has been judged as less dispensable than cooperative ideals. The partnership has no doubt ensured that target groups and institutions had to comply with introduced measures and hence, also, an acceptable implementation record. In terms of impact rather than implementation performance, however, the longer term achievements leave much to be desired. As a matter of fact, the main contribution of the support rendered seems to have been to strengthen an institutional set-up in which primary societies have been reduced to mere appendices to central and regional bureaucracies.

Apart from direct resource transfers, assistance has tended to confine itself to find technically feasible solutions to administrative and organizational issues. Within this context, high priority has been given 'supply-side strategies'. Lack of credit and inputs have been perceived as critical constraints to growth of agricultural production. As noted by von Pischke et. al., one attractive feature of credit programmes is their "appearance of offering fast relief for complex situations" (1983:2). They are easier and, not least, cheaper to introduce than land reforms, investments in infrastructure and other measures aimed at raising the production capacity of the rural economy.

That the bureaucratic government-controlled mode developed for introducing input intensive technologies eventually would turn defunct could have been anticipated, had social information been gathered and used more systematically. A common feature of external assistance thus is that it has not been preceded by sufficiently serious attempts to appraise social and economic implications of either national development policies or the strategies and institutional machinery devised for rural, agricultural and cooperative development. Prior to the design of supporting measures it would of course in most cases also have been necessary to examine the local environments in which support is intended with regard to agro-ecology, infrastructure, landownership, education and, not least, farmers' preferences and priorities.

CONCLUSIONS

First it has to be noted that our empirical findings rather consistently support the conclusion that farmers respond to economic incentives. The problem is that these incentives are a function not only of prices and competition, but also of 'residual' circumstances which profoundly affect conditions of production and consumption. Kenya represents a case where both markets and 'residual' factors have been subjected to a combined mode of state intervention that has seriously distorted the development of smallholder agriculture.

Thus, the neglect of the need for infrastructural support has resulted in inadequate and regionally biased investments in public goods. Second, government has permeated the expanding market system with an inordinate range of laws, regulations and administrative structures. In rural environments characterized by low productivity and high distance friction, the structure and behaviour prescribed for cooperatives have created unrealistic threshold requirements and made their management excessively dependent on spatially extended networks of decision-making and supervision. This has seriously obstructed not only the democratic features usually associated with cooperatives but also largely eliminated essential ingredients of entrepreneurship such as creativity, flexibility and adaptability.

Furthermore, a continued and widening mismatch between environmental requirements and the prescribed mode of cooperative organization can be expected. Shortage of arable land in combination with rapid population growth will perpetuate land fragmentation. In this setting, the cost of supplying services through administratively demanding cooperatives will become prohibitive. Hence societies will either cease to operate, or they will have to depend increasingly on government subsidies, or confine their services to narrow strata of commercial farmers.

State intervention has also come to play the additional twin roles of facilitating appropriation/diversion of financial resources for the benefit of privileged strata, and of exercising political control. These features have become more pronounced following the reorientation of agricultural service cooperatives towards 'supply-side' functions, i.e. the administered provision of credit and farm inputs.

Large portions of the cooperative structure thus can be seen as part of a cob web of legitimated privileges that cause petrification of the social reproduction process of the economy at large. Hence it effectively contributes to the exclusion of private initiatives which in minor or major ways threaten established political or economic interests. What might the remedy be? Given the present context, one probable course would be to resort to some kind of 'muddle through' strategy, including the following rectifying measures:

(1)   Liberalize national marketing systems for agricultural produce.

(2)   Reorganize primary and secondary societies.

   (a)   Abolish the present administrative system which integrates marketing, credit and input supplies, and abolish credit sales to individual members.

   (b)   Separate savings/credit activities from unions - and allow independent cooperative organizaions to deal with these services.

   (c)   Give priority to efficient marketing services at the primary level, with emphasis on collection, delivery and payments. Stimulate the establishment of multiproduce societies and, in particular, the inclusion of marketing services for staple (food) produce.

(3)   Intensify and decentralize management training of committee members and union/society staff.

(4)   Reorganize and intensify member/committee member education.

(5)   Revise/liberalize cooperative legislation.

(6) These measures will have to be preceded or at least combined with radically increased public investment in infrastructure, including rural service centres.

As regards the list of needed changes in the cooperative sector, it could certainly be made both longer and more detailed. The catch, however, is that in the medium term the suggested measures are constrained by the mode of cooperative development of which they now constitute part. First it is questionable if the government, with the support of donor agencies, would manage to implement these kinds of revised policies in line with underlying intentions (Sandbrook 1985). Second, even if implementation succeeds, basic stratification mechanisms may not be affected (Leys 1975). Third, if the present legislation is not changed, possible positive impacts would be neutralized by a sustained dysfunctionality between commercial efficiency requirements and state administration. In this respect, organization theory supports our conclusion that multi-level organizational structures cannot accommodate both differentiation among base units and a high degree of vertical interdependence (Lorsch and Allen 1973). Hence, there is little reason to be very optimistic about the outcome of a revised cooperative development strategy.

It is therefore more probable that the present development strategy, with its reliance on bureaucratic superstructures and administrative engineering, will remain largely intact. Within this context, incremental benefits are likely to be appropriated by the establishment and a narrow stratum of the smallholder population, on terms determined by the former. To most smallholders this would mean continued limited access to adequate production and marketing services, and the national economy would suffer both in terms of efficiency and allocation.

With greater priority given to what would be advantageous to the rural economy in general and smallholders in particular, rather than to the survival of the present type of cooperatives, a different set of measures seems to be called for, inter alia:

* abolish license arrangements and monopolies in wholesale and manufacturing;
* deregulate the national market system for agricultural produce and inputs;
* vitiate, or at least drastically reduce the role of, national marketing boards;
* revoke local monopolies, including those of cooperatives, i.e. allow private traders to participate freely in marketing and input supply activities; and

* replace the present cooperative law with legislation that protects cooperative societies from government intervention.

As in the case of the 'muddle through' scenario above, a drastic reorientation of priorities regarding public investment in infrastructure to the advantage of rural areas and smallholder agriculture would be necessary. This would include investment in transports, rural service centres, extension services, research focussing on the requirements of smallholders, water supplies, health, education, land rehabilitation and conservation. Government thus should attend to its conventional raison d'etre, namely the provision of public goods. It would also be within this realm that donor agencies could make useful contributions. Donor agency interventions through integrated rural development programmes conventionally involve resource transfers of 'private goods' character. These, however, have to be avoided as they typically result in market distortions and serious social anomalies.

Arguments in favour of economic liberalization and de-regulation are thus not a matter only of competition and prices, although those aspects in themselves are important. The decisive importance of liberalization lies more in the fact that it is not compatible with political repression, and therefore will enhance levels of social activity, including intensified circulation of information and economic interaction. Hence, it will also release/develop resources in the form of initiative, knowledge, experience and ambitions among ordinary people who under the present system are petrified by fear, apathy and defaitism.

The impact of these changes can be expected to be significant. At least in the short or medium term, one effect would be a drastically reduced number of active agricultural service societies. In the new setting most of the marketing and input supply services would probably be taken over by more efficient and flexible private enterprises. At least in part, these effects would directly benefit the smallholder. Adding the consequences of changed legislation, the role of the ministry and central bureaus would diminish. The role of the government bureaucracy could be confined to what conventionally is expected by a 'Registrar of cooperatives', i.e. registration of societies and a general control that cooperatives operate in accordance with basic laws of book-keeping.

How then would the suggested changes affect smallholders in terms of bargaining position and democratic participation? As regards the latter aspect, it is clear that within the present institutional setting the influence of members/smallholders on cooperatives is minimal. This is due both to the bureaucracy and regulations emanating from the cooperative legislation, and to the political and economic system of which they constitute part. Liberalization of the economy would strengthen individual freedom and, hence, facilitate increased voluntary participation in local associations, farmers' unions, etc.

If a liberalized market leads to cartels and generally unfavorable bargains for farmers in their dealings with the commercial sector, they have in the new context an option that does not exist today, namely that of utilizing organizational means for strengthening their position. These means include not only farmers' unions but certainly also the establishment of service cooperatives. As distinct from the present situation they would then be cooperative not only by name but also in nature by emanating from and being governed by local, commonly felt needs.

LITERATURE

Bates, R. (1981) *Markets and States in Tropical Africa: The Political Basis of Agricultural Policies.* University of California Press, Berkely.

Gyllström, B. (1986) *Government vs. Agricultural Marketing Co-operatives in Kenya.* Some Observations on Modes and Consequences of State Intervention. Paper presented at the seminar "Co-operatives Revisited". The Scandinavian Institute of African Studies, Uppsala.

Harvey, C., Jacobs, J., Lamb, G., Schaeffer, B. (1979) *Rural Employment and Administration in the Third World. Development Methods and Alternative Strategies.* Saxon House.

Hedenmalm, Å. (1985) *Farmers' Unions and Rural Development.* The Case of Kenya National Farmers' Union. Geografiska inst., University of Umeå.

Hedlund, H. (1986) *Kaffe, Kooperation och Kultur. En studie av en kooperativ kaffeförening i Kibirigwi, Kenya.* Nordiska Afrikainstitutet, Uppsala.

Hydén, G. (1973) *Efficiency vs. Distribution in East African Co-operatives. A Study in Organizational Conflicts.* East African Literature Bureau, Nairobi.

Hydén, G. (1983) *No Shortcuts to Progress. African Development Management in Perspective.* Heinemann, London.

Ilchman W.F. and Bhargava R.C. (1973) 'Balanced Thought and Economic Growth', pp. 26-44 in C.K. Wilber (ed.) *The Political Economy of Development and Underdevelopment.* Random House, New York.

ILO (1972) *Employment, Incomes and Equality. A strategy for increasing productive employment in Kenya.* ILO, Geneva.

Karanja, E. (1974) *The Development of Co-operative Movement in Kenya*. Ph.D. thesis, University of Pittsburg.

Kitching, G. (1980) *Class and Economic Change in Kenya. The Making of an African Petite-Bourgeoisie*, Yale University.

Lamb, G. (1974) 'Government, Co-operatives and Peasant Agriculture in Kenya'. *IDS Bulletin*, Vol.6, No.1.

Leo, C. (1984) *Land and Class in Kenya*. University of Toronto Press, Toronto.

Leys, C. (1975) *Underdevelopment in Kenya. The Political Economy of Neo-Colonialism 1964-71*. Heinemann, London.

Lorsch, J.W. and Allen, S.A. (1975) *Managing Diversity and Interdependence*. Harvard University, Boston.

Njonjo, A., Chege, F., Kimenye, D., Ng'ang'a, A. (1985) *Final Report on Co-operative Production Credit Scheme Study*. Business and Economic Research Co. Ltd., Nairobi.

Ouma, S. (1980) *A History of the Co-operative Movement in Kenya*. Bookwise Ltd., Nairobi.

von Pischke, J.D., Adams, D.W., Donald, G. (1983) *Rural Financial Markets in Developing Countries. Their Use and Abuse*. The John Hopkins University Press, Baltimore.

Republic of Kenya (1970) *Sessional Paper No.8 1970*. Government Printer. Nairobi.

Samuelsson, M. (1987) *Womens' Ability to Participate Actively in Co-operatives*. Dep. of Social and Economic Geography, University of Lund (stencil).

Sandbrook, R. (1985) *The Politics of Africa's Economic Stagnation._*Cambridge University Press, Cambridge.

Soja, E.W. (1968) *The Geography of Modernization in Kenya. A Spatial Analysis of Social, Economic and Political Change*. Syracuse University Press.

Standa, E.M., Maranga, J.S. (1981) *The Cooperative Member and Committee Member Education Programme*. Report No.7. Research and Evaluation Unit, Ministry of Co-operative Development, Nairobi.

Svensson, B. (1986) In Hedlund (1986) *Kaffe kooperation och kultur. En studie av en kooperativ kafferförening i Kibirigwi, Kenya.* Nordiska Afrikainstitutet, Uppsala.

Widstrand, C-G. (1972) 'Problems of Efficiency in the Performance of Co-operatives', pp. 9-31 in Widstrand, C.G.(ed.) *African Co-operatives and Efficiency.* The Scandinavian Institute of African Studies, Uppsala.

Worsley, P. (1971) *Two Blades of Grass. Rural Co-operatives in Agricultural Modernization.* Manchester University Press.

van Zwanenberg, R.W.A. (1975) *An Economic History of Kenya and Uganda.* The MacMillan Press Ltd., London.

CHAPTER 2

CAPTURING THE PEASANTS THROUGH COOPERATIVES - THE CASE
OF ETHIOPIA

by Michael Ståhl

INTRODUCTION

The image of Ethiopia in the West is one of ecological degradation, starvation
and war. Population growth, in the absence of technological change, causes
heavy pressure on arable land by cultivation and grazing. Vegetation is
relentlessly removed and erosion is rampant. Crop yields decline and peasant
reserves dwindle. When drought strikes, the scene is set for disaster[1].
Rehabilitation and emergency aid is made difficult due to the civil strife which
haunts the northern highlands.

It is easily forgotten that there are high potential agricultural regions which
have good enough soils and receive ample precipitation to secure relatively high
yields of cereal crops. These regions include primarily the highlands of Arsi,
Shoa and Gojjam. In addition to feeding a peasant population of some twelve
million people these regions produce two thirds of the officially marketed grain
in the country[2]. Peasant agriculture in these central regions form the backbone
of Ethiopia's attempts to thwart the present trend towards dependence on food
aid for survival[3].

What is being done to develop peasant agriculture in these high potential
regions? Throughout the 1980s the Ethiopian authorities and Western donors
funding rural development programmes have been involved in a debate on
development strategies. While the donors argue in favour of strengthening the
private smallholder sector, the Ethiopian authorities promote a 'transition to
socialism' focussing on collective solutions in production and trade[4].

In a recent article Cohen and Isaksson survey the debate on alternative
strategies for food production in Ethiopia and review the effects on production
of collectivist agricultural policies[5]. While providing a useful overview of the
policy issues involved, the article argues at a general level and invites a more
detailed discussion.

ETHIOPIA

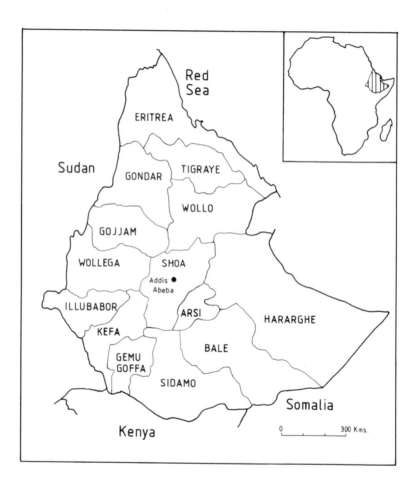

The purpose of this paper is to further explore the actual functioning of service and producers' cooperatives, the two major agricultural institutions set up by the authorities in order to increase peasant production and transform it along socialist lines. The presentation centres on the motives for and character of state intervention in peasant agriculture utilizing these two organizations.

The title of the paper alludes to Göran Hydén's well known analysis of African peasantries. He argues that the African states face problems managing the rural economy because the peasants live in their own world. They are 'uncaptured' by the state. If agricultural policies do not favour them, the peasants have the option of withdrawing into subsistence production regulated by the informal 'economy of affection' where they are free from state control[6]. Hydén draws on field material mainly from Kenya and Tanzania but he considers his argument to be relevant throughout Sub-Saharan Africa.

This paper can be read with Hydén's argumentation in mind. It shows that the Ethiopian state has the organizational capacity of capturing the peasantry and extracting tributes from it. The impressive institution-building carried out after the revolution and involving service and producers' cooperatives, parastatal procurement of grain, villagization and resettlement, can be viewed as a gigantic and successful attempt to capture the peasants. While this can be demonstrated, the question is whether the attempt is successful in terms of the first priority of official agricultural policy - to produce enough food. This question is discussed in the concluding remarks.

The Ethiopian scholar Abraham Demoz said that Ethiopia is the despair of the compulsive classifier[7]. The argumentation in this paper is certainly not representative of peasant society and agricultural policy throughout the highlands. The empirical material is drawn primarily from Arsi, Shoa and Gojjam - regions[8] where people do not starve, infrastructure is comparatively developed, government is in firm control and the peasants have learned to comply with officialdom[9].

RURAL ORGANIZATIONS

Before proceeding to the subject matter the organizations which will figure throughout the ensuing discussion will be introduced. They include the Peasant Association, the Service Cooperative and the Producers Cooperative. They were created after the revolution and are established institutions in the rural areas. Other mass organizations include the Revolutionary Ethiopian Women's Association and the Revolutionary Ethiopian Youth Association. The village is a recent administrative innovation.

The legal underpinnings and general operations of the peasant associations, service cooperatives and producers' cooperatives have been described and analyzed by a number of scholars[10]. Hence, only a brief review will be undertaken here so as to provide the background for a more detailed discussion.

The *Peasant Association* (PA) is the basic rural institution in post-revolutionary Ethiopia. Initially created for the purposes of defeating the landlords and abolishing the feudal system, the PAs are now semi-official administrative units at the grass root level. The PA is a territorial organization encompassing 800 hectares or more. All peasant households living in the area should be members. In actual fact many peasant households remain outside the PAs although the great majority are members. The average PA membership is 150 - 300 households. All arable areas in regions under state control are covered with a network of PAs. Their total number is some 20,000. The PA members constitute an assembly which gathers a few times a year. It elects a chairman and an executive committee which run the daily affairs of the association. In addition the assembly elects a judicial tribunal which functions as a local court, deciding in minor legal matters. There are sub-committees attached to the executive committee to deal with matters such as defence/security, administrative affairs and development. Government, local administration and the Workers Party of Ethiopia get in touch with the peasant population through the PAs. Information on new directives and proclamations, development campaigns, public work etc. is transmitted to the population and implemented by the PAs. They also mobilize labour for tree planting and soil conservation programmes. During drought they are vehicles for distribution of food aid.

A major function of PAs has been to allocate land to member households. In the first few years after revolution, this included ousting of landlords and corrections of gross inequalities in access to land. The principle adhered to is that land should be distributed equally, adjustments being made for household size. No household is entitled to have more than 10 ha according to the land reform proclamation. In actual practise the size of holdings average 0.5 - 4 ha depending on the local situation. Redistribution is in theory a continuous process, the aim of which is to make sure that the increasing households have access to agricultural land. Actually, redistribution at the PA level takes place only after consent by political authorities through the Ministry of Agriculture. In Gondar and Gojjam the last general redistribution took place in 1980.

The authorities have charged PAs with the function of collecting taxes. Individual peasant households pay a land tax (ETB 10) and an income tax (minimum ETB 20).

The PAs are organized vertically at all administrative levels (sub-district, district, region) and also form an apex organization called All Ethiopian

Peasants Association (AEPA). Leaders at a lower level elect representatives to the level above. The AEPA chairman is member of the Central Committee of the Workers' Party. However, the higher PA units do not function as interest groups for their grass root organizations. They appear rather to be supportive of the administration[11].

The *Service Cooperative* (SC) is composed of three to ten PAs. As the name implies its function is to render services to member associations. Households have to pay an initial membership fee of ETB 5-15. The PA chairman represents his association at SC meetings. The SC has a chairman and an executive committee. Some SCs also employ staff - bookkeepers and shop attendants. Most SCs run a cooperative shop where basic consumer goods (salt, sugar, matches, soap, coffee, blankets etc.) are retailed when available from the Ethiopian Domestic Distribution Corporation (EDDC).

Another function of the SC is purchase of grain from peasants in the member PAs. The SC stores the grain and sells it to the state purchasing agent, the Agricultural Marketing Corporation (AMC). Prices are set by the Ministry of Domestic Trade. The SC get a margin of ETB 5 per quintal (100 kg) for its procurement service. The SC buys a quintal of wheat from a peasant at a price of ETB 35 and sells it to AMC at a price of ETB 40. The funds thus accumulated are utilized for various development projects or given as loans to member PAs in accordance with rules. In recent years an increasing number of SCs have started to distribute agricultural inputs to peasants in their member PAs. This was previously a function of the Ministry of Agriculture (MOA). Under the arrangement fertilizer and certified seed are procured by the Agricultural Inputs Supply Corporation (AISCO) and forwarded to SCs for distribution to members in accordance with a credit scheme. This arrangement is being tried in the surplus producing regions of Arsi, Shoa and Gojjam. The system is yet to be fully elaborated and it demands skilled manpower at the SC level to cater for logistical and accounting tasks. There are some 4,500 SCs in Ethiopia.

The original intention behind the SCs was to strengthen peasants' bargaining power vz. the private grain merchants. The situation has changed gradually. When the government started to push for a state monopoly position in the field of grain trade the role of SCs has increasingly become that of subordinate counterparts to the state procurement agency.

The major purpose of *Producers' Cooperatives* (PC) is to promote collective farming. The political authorities look upon PCs as spearheads for socialist transformation on the countryside. A PC can be created by a small group within a PA. More details about the PCs will be given in the analysis which follows. In 1986 there were slightly less than 2,000 PCs with a total membership of some 130,000 or around 2% of all peasant households.

The *village* is a newly added institution which is officially promoted. Traditionally the Ethiopian peasantry live in scattered homesteads in between fields and pastures. Small clusters of houses can be found occasionally. Since the late 1970s the official policy is to urge people to settle in villages of a more concentrated character. In 1985 comprehensive villagization was announced in the Arsi region. Each PA was to choose a site for settlement of its members. The existing houses were dismantled, moved to the village site and rebuilt there. Villagization was scheduled for the dry season months December-March. The Workers' Party of Ethiopia, the regional administration and the Ministry of Agriculture assisted Peasant Associations to move. Villagization was an order given by the highest political authority. Rather efficiently implemented, some 70% of the peasant households in the Arsi region did in fact move into villages in 1985/86[12]. The following year villagization proceeded in several other regions. It grew into a national campaign. Detailed regulations for its implementation have been issued[13]. Villagization is the most far-reaching structural change implemented in Ethiopia so far. It signifies a complete break with the traditional peasant logic of living and producing. It is interesting to note, though, that there are already reports of peasants quietly moving back to their old homesteads, while retaining the house in the village, which they occasionally visit. An analysis of villagization goes beyond the scope of this article. In the concluding remarks the consequences of villagization on collective agriculture and socialization of grain trade will be commented on.

THE POLITICAL CONTEXT

A few notes on the official Ethiopian rural development strategy will be made to put the analysis in context.

The military government, which replaced Haile Selassie, and its ideological wing, the Workers Party of Ethiopia (WPE), favour collective solutions in agricultural development. This bias stems from two sources, one political and one economic/technical.

The imperial regime was an expression of and gave its staunch support to the class of landlords. The landlords were a "feudal" class deriving their wealth from corvee labour, service obligations and rent in cash and kind from tenants and share-croppers living on their land. Starting in the 1960s a progressive element amongst the landlords emerged. These people moved into agricultural production themselves, evicting tenants in order to create viable mechanized, commercial farms. The agricultural policy at that time favoured commercial production through credits and subsidies on, inter alia, tractors and fuel. A number of wealthy peasants as well as rich townspeople also managed to take advantage of the credits and invested in mechanized production[14].

During the revolution the feudal landlords, capitalist farmers and rich peasants were singled out as 'counterrevolutionaries'. The revolutionary government prohibited individual large scale agriculture and the engagement of hired labour in peasant agriculture, it destroyed the emerging class of agrarian capitalists and harassed its members. The revolutionaries had great plans for the poor peasants and the tenants. In the new socialist oriented society which was to emerge, these underprivileged groups would function as a proletarian, collectivist vanguard, it was thought.

This ideology has been cemented over time. It has gone so far that individual (family based) agriculture is suspect in the eyes of the political authorities. The ideologists think that individual peasants might evolve into capitalist farmers. Individually based agricultural production should therefore be officially discouraged. On the other hand, the Producers Cooperatives are seen as spearheads for collectivization of peasant agriculture. PCs should thus be given maximum official support. To criticize the actual performance of PCs is considered a counterrevolutionary act.

The economic/technical considerations for collective agricultural production are the following. The political authorities have repeatedly lamented the backwardness of Ethiopian peasants. This is done in political speeches and massmedia. Truly, a television zoom-in on a rugged peasant leaning against his old fashioned plough and shouting at his skinny oxen presents no progressive view. It is believed that the peasants are hopelessly backward and that nothing less than a profound break with traditions would open their minds to modernization. Producers Cooperatives are considered to be the instrument through which peasant conservatism can be overcome.

A technical argument in favour of PCs is the fragmented character of the agricultural landscape. Arable land is divided into minute plots and each household has several such plots often with long distances in between. The PAs have a thorough knowledge of where the good, mediocre and poor agricultural soils are situated within their area. For reasons of justice and equality, each household is entitled to portions of land of different fertility categories. Population increase also necessitates periodic subdivisions of holdings in order to accommodate new households. Every PA member has a legal right to arable land. Land cannot be private property but all PA members have rights to use land. As a result of these processes agricultural land is fragmented. The authorities argue that through the formation of Producers Cooperatives, pooling of land becomes possible and thereby the establishment of large, economically viable production units which render themselves to mechanization.

EMERGENCE OF COLLECTIVE FARMING

Already in the earliest official documents and guide-lines on agriculture issued after the revolution, there were references to group farming[15]. Among the tasks given to the newly established Peasant Associations promotion of collective farms is mentioned. During the "Development through Cooperation Campaign" peasants were encouraged to set aside communal land for collective cultivation.

A great number of communal land plots thus emerged in the mid 1970s. Most of them encompassed only a few hectares. Their purpose was often to raise a cash crop in order to give the PA money to invest in various small projects. But uncertainty prevailed regarding the development of collective farming. Rules regarding work input and distribution of harvests were never clarified. Most peasants concentrated their efforts on their family farms. Collective farms therefore remained a residual, cultural practices and yields being below the standard of family farms[16]. The authorities, which were considering how to move fast in the socialist direction, realized that as long as peasants were involved both in family and group farming, the former production units would receive the bulk of work input. Consequently, group farms would show poor results and thus jeopardize socialist progress.

COOPERATIVE HIERARCHY

In 1979 the authorities changed approach. The new policy was to promote group farming as the sole form of production among nucleus peasant collectives which were to be established within the PAs. A 'Directive on the Establishment of Producers Cooperatives' was issued in 1979 providing guide-lines for the systematic promotion of group farming[17]. A new organizational form of agricultural production was thereby formally sanctioned. It was named "Agricultural Producers Cooperative" (PC).

The philosophy underlying the directive is that once a small group of peasants has formed a cooperative, it would receive extension advice and preferential access to inputs by the Ministry of Agriculture (MOA). Extension would focus on modernization of agricultural production along collective lines. By virtue of the expected superior yields emanating from group farms, more peasants would become attracted to the idea and join the PC. The final goal is that all members of the PA would join the cooperative. Eventually peasant agriculture would change completely from small scale, family based production to large scale, collective production.

It may be of interest to describe the process of collective transformation, as it is outlined in policy documents.

According to the directive, a minimum of three PA members can decide to apply to MOA for assistance to form a PC. MOA visits the PA and assesses the potential of the presumptive cooperative. Applications are never turned down, only postponed when MOA lacks manpower to assist them. Once a PC has been formed inside a PA no other agricultural cooperative can be formed there. Peasants who become interested in collective production may join the existing PC. When membership has reached 30 the PC can apply for formal registration. It then becomes eligible for loans from official credit institutions.

In the first stage of collectivization PC members pool only agricultural land, roughly 0.5 to 2 ha per member. Draught-oxen, tools and other inputs remain private property, but the PC is entitled to rent tools and oxen from members. This stage is called *malba* in the official terminology. The purpose is that the PC as soon as possible should proceed to the second stage of collectivization, *welba*. Here, oxen, ploughs and other implements are turned into collective property. Individual plots are allowed to a maximum size of 0.1 hectare.

The PC assumes a more organized form at the *welba* stage. Collective operations may be broadened to include animal husbandry as well as services such as grain milling. An elaborate work organization is needed to cope with the different collective tasks. The Ministry of Agriculture has issued regulations related to the division of work and remuneration to PC members for tasks performed. The general principle is that work-points are given to members on a time rate. Work is also classified according to its drudgery; eight hours work behind the plough gives more work-points than eight hours of bird-scaring in the fields. However, it has been difficult to include quality of work into the remuneration system. Book-keeping becomes a necessity due to the need to account for collective economic activities, plan for investments and distribute benefits to members[18].

The traditional settlement pattern in the Ethiopian countryside is scattered. With increasing cooperative membership in a Peasant Association, with more complex cooperative undertakings and with emerging cooperative economic and social services (grain milling, kindergarten, clinic), the need for a concentration of the residential pattern amongst PC members becomes evident. PCs in the *welba* stage established villages, with generous assistance from MOA, already in the early 1980s[19].

The third stage of collectivization is called *weland* in the official terminology. A *weland* may be formed through merging a few *welbas*. This stage presupposes advanced farming methods including mechanization, comprehensive economic and social services and complete villagization. This is the highest form of collectivization and the description of it in propaganda posters leads thought to the now defunct Chinese People's Communes.

In late 1987 one third of the PCs had reached the more advanced *welba* stage. To date no *weland* has been created.

The members of a PC constitute an assembly which elects a chairman, a management committee and a supervisory committee. The function of the latter is to set criteria for remuneration of work, to assign duties to work-teams and to record their performance (give work points to each member).

The formation of PCs include, in the official Ethiopian development policy, much more than group farming. The planners and party ideologues envisage a new way of life evolving whereby peasants gradually adopt a socialist culture. The material basis of that culture would be the experiences of collective work and collective services which, theoretically, are supposed to enhance productivity and welfare. The PAs are considered to be temporary organizations. When all PA members have joined the PC, the collective would become the basic rural organization at the grass root level.

ISSUES FOR DISCUSSION

The presentation can now proceed to problematize the following issues related to PCs: social recruitment, state subsidies and production potential.

Who join PCs?

The directive on Producers Cooperatives and the ensuing propaganda to create PCs was received with hesitation by the peasant population. Often it was interpreted as an attempt by the government to separate the households from their means of production and make them "work for the state". Such an attitude was logical among the established households, i.e. those with relatively good land and access to draught oxen. The directive was welcomed by very poor households, i.e. those having agricultural fields on marginal land and lacking draught oxen and the semi-proletarianized households on the fringes of peasant associations. For such people, joining a PC could be an instrument to gain access to productive agricultural resources. The directive thus carried a seed of conflict into the peasant associations that was to grow when the authorities started to push implementation.

In order to continue this line of argument it may be of interest to try to reconstruct the early stages of cooperative formation with regard to internal relations in the PAs and the influence of local authorities[20].

The founding members of PCs were often "lumpen-proletarians" or heads of households with very meagre resources. Many had tenant and share-cropper status before the revolution. Some were former tenants who had been evicted by landlords and forced to move away. After the revolution they turned back to their native areas only to find that the land was already reallocated by the PAs.

The first step in collectivization is to pool members' land. If the founding members lived scattered throughout the PA territory, reshuffling of agricultural land was necessary in order to make room for a uniform collective field. In the densely populated highlands all agricultural land of good quality is already in use. Therefore the authorities had to create a rule allowing PC members to choose a piece of land anywhere in the PA territory which could accommodate their collective farming needs. Those peasants who happened to live and farm in the area chosen by the PC, had to move. They were given the choice of taking over the fields which the PC members had abandoned or seek virgin land, if available. It is evident that such reallocations were resisted by the peasantry at large. The PC members chose the best land of course in sharp contrast with their previous family plots which were often rocky and worn out. The early PC members utilized the new rules and directives on collective farming in order to expand their farming resources at the expense of better-off PA members. It is important to note that the authorities gave administrative and economic support to this process, thus openly siding with the poorest social strata in their struggle over resources within PAs.

It happened that the authorities handed out guns to PC members so that they could protect the emerging collective from the wrath of peasants being separated from their ancestral land as a result of the reshuffling of plots. The directive on PC formation stipulated that once a PC had been created the chairmanship of the whole Peasant Association had to be vested in a member of the PC. The defence squad which exists in every PA was also composed in such a manner that the PC controlled it.

The interference in favour of PCs tended to alienate the majority of peasants from the collective endeavour[21].

The actual nature of the growth of PC membership deserves further study[22]. An interesting notion is that the growth of membership in many places is due to creation of new PCs in ever more PAs, rather than to an increase of membership in existing PCs. One pattern is that a PC is established by a dozen individuals. Membership grows quickly to 40-50 households whereafter it remains fairly constant. This pattern of fast initial growth followed by stagnation opens up interesting hypotheses for research. In discussions with cooperative promotion officials one comes across the argument that such PCs consist of a core group which, once established, is reluctant to accept additional members on a large scale. The reason would be that they want to monopolize the privileges and support received from the authorities. Some of these privileges are exploitative in nature, as will be shown below. In such cases the PC emerges as a closely knit interest group, often based on primordial loyalties, benefiting from official support and their power to exploit non-members (this requires that strong personalities are in control of the PC). If all households in the Peasant Association would join the cooperative, its privileged position would be diluted.

Another pattern is that after some years of wait-and-see, the great majority of peasants join and are welcomed by the founding members. Such a trend could be noticed in Ticho in 1986, which will be discussed below.

Yet another pattern is when the strong and established households form a PC and leave the elderly and weak PA members outside. "Why should we let those people in", they argue, "they are too weak to work and would only consume".

The position of women in PCs is unclear. Only the head of household can be PC member. The peasant wife is therefore excluded. Still she is supposed to work on the collective field to help her husband. Whatever she gets out of such work depends on the relations within the household. In many parts of Ethiopia women inherit land and own livestock. When the head of household joins a PC, land and livestock are collectivized. The wife thereby looses her private assets without gaining membership. Her position in society is devalued. There are many gender aspects in cooperative formation which remain unsolved. These aspects would merit attention by the Revolutionary Ethiopian Women's Association.

The different social patterns mentioned above are mere outlines. Systematic research would undoubtedly reveal interesting social constellations.

State subsidies to PCs

The official status given to Producers Cooperatives means that they are supported in various ways by MOA and the local party and administration offices. The following list of privileges has been compiled during discussions with officials in various positions[23].

(i) PCs pay lower *tax*. While individual peasants pay ETB 10 per year, PC members pay ETB 5 per year.

(ii) PCs receive preferential treatment when *fertilizer* and certified seed are distributed on *credit*.

(iii) PCs enjoy *concessionary prices*, up to 12% cheaper than individual peasants, when buying agricultural inputs from the Agricultural Marketing Corporation.

(iv) MOA *extension service* gives priority to PCs regarding agronomic advice, preparation of farm plans, artificial insemination and general veterinary services, distribution of beehives, cross-bred cattle etc.

(v) PCs are entitled to utilize 25% of the annual net surplus generated by the Service Cooperative where they are members as a *low-interest loan.*

(vi) Once a PC is formed inside a *PA*, the *chairmanship* of the whole Peasant Association is transferred to a member of the PC.

(vii) PC members are sometimes armed with *guns* by the authorities and assume the security function for the whole Peasant Association.

(viii) Local authorities can persuade the Service Cooperative to use their capital to buy *heavy machinery*, e.g. a tractor or - in rare cases - a combine harvester, for rental to members. Since only the PC cultivates fields large enough to fit mechanized harvesting, the PC(s) inside the Service Cooperative area monopolizing use of such machinery. The rent paid by the PC to the SC only includes costs for fuel, lubricants and driver's daily allowance. Thus, amortization of the bank loan taken by the SC to buy the combine is paid by all SC members although only a small minority has any use of it.

(ix) Local authorities can instruct all members of a Peasant Association to assist the PC to carry out farm operations during peak agricultural seasons (ploughing, weeding, harvesting).

(x) Local authorities can instruct all Peasant Association members to provide daily labour to PC special projects (building an office or a clinic for the PC members).

(xi) PCs receive gifts from the state during visits by high ranking officials. Such gifts can include a diesel pump, a tractor, corrugated iron roofs for residential houses etc.

(xii) The authorities systematically direct grants for rural development purposes (water supplies, irrigation schemes, social services) given by international donors so that they primarily benefit PCs.

(xiii) Sons of PC members are not drafted into the national military service. The service lasts for two years. After six months of training the conscripts join the professional army fighting guerilla and secessionist groups in different parts of the country. This regulation appears to be practised in some districts, while it is unknown in others.

While some of the privileges mentioned above imply subsidies by the state and donors, others imply an official sanction for the PC to exploit the labour of individual members (notably v, viii, ix and x). This is done quite consciously by the government for two reasons. One is to boost the productive resources of the PCs and thereby help them "take off" economically. The other reason is to show that individual farming has less official support, and that, in consequence, peasants who want to benefit from government policies must join PCs.

The nature of official agitation

The voluntariness of cooperative formation is sometimes questioned by outside observers. One fact should be kept in mind. People must apply for membership and they must pay a fee in order to be admitted to a PC. In some cases the established PC members hesitate to admit new members. With the exception of the forced collectivization in the Wabe district in Arsi in the late 1970s, there has not been any organized coercive official campaign to force peasants en masse into PCs[24]. But it is well known that the highest political authority has set an ambitious target for PC expansion. According to the ten year development plan, 53% of the peasant households are supposed to have joined PCs by 1993[25].

The administration proceeds with subtle means to promote cooperative formation. At the local administrative level pressure is exercised on peasants to abandon their traditional way of life and join or form a PC. The government encourages local authorities to set up annual targets for increase in cooperative membership within their area of administrative responsibility. The pressure is thus first felt on the administrators. Setting a very modest target would be considered reactionary and the responsible official might face accusations of being a counterrevolutionary. Local administrators are usually keen to set ambitious targets for cooperative formation. The targets are formally set in the form of quotas; X number of new PCs will be formed and Y number of new members to new and old PCs will be recruited. In the Arsi region local authorities have throughout the 1980s set the most ambitious target - 10% increase in total membership per annum. Most years they have exceeded this target[26].

Party and administration officials as well as MOA staff transfer the pressure down to the peasants. The instruments at hand include positive and negative sanctions (see the above list), in particular the appropriation of labour from neighbouring individual peasants. This is highly attractive since it can remove bottle-necks demanding much drudgery during the agricultural peak season. It is prohibited by law to employ farm labour in peasant agriculture. Claiming that the individual peasants just help the PC, while actually they are forced to work on PC farms, is a way of circumventing the law. It is also a clear message to the individual peasants that PCs have the backing of the state.

Agitation is part of the picture. Party officials and administrators tour the countryside giving lectures on the merits of socialism, indicating that the whole world is now turning towards this system. Also MOA field staff who are supposed to carry out agricultural extension work, are dragged into the ideological apparatus. Development agents often complain that they have too little time to carry out their professional tasks due to propaganda tasks imposed on them by the local administrator or party official.

It is tempting for the authorities to use MOA field staff for agitation purposes, because MOA is, together with the Ministry of Education, the ministry which has the most elaborate staffing at the lowest administrative levels. It should be noted how the term "agitation" is defined in Ethiopia today. It means that all positive aspects of a given phenomenon (collectivization, villagization, resettlement etc.) are explained and even exaggerated to the peasants while possible negative aspects are overlooked.

Agricultural potential of PCs

The discussion can now proceed to the question of whether collective farms are more productive than individual peasant farms. Snapshots from two famous PCs may serve as an introduction.

Huruta Hetosa is a well known Producers Cooperative, frequently visited by prominent people. It is officially registered and has some 250 member households of which 15% are headed by women. On the high plateau of the Arsi region, the cooperative cultivates 400 ha collectively. Main crops are wheat, barley, teff and maize. Onions are grown on irrigated land. The members built a village long before the official villagization campaign started. In the village there are services such as grain and oil milling, piped water supply, electricity and a kindergarten. The cooperative owns 200 draught oxen and two tractors. Together with a neighbouring PC, Huruta Hetosa owns a combine harvester. It received a seed cleaner from the UN Capital Development Fund. In addition to collective efforts, members grow vegetables in small home gardens.

The general impression is one of prosperity. Member incomes are well above the national average. A considerable part of income derives from the small but efficiently run irrigated onion fields. Onions are marketed in the nearby market town of Nazareth at a price of ETB 0.7 per kg, which is almost twice the official price for grain.

The yield of cereal fields per hectare is not that impressive, considering all available inputs. During 1981-86 it averaged 1.9 metric tons per hectare. Nearby individual peasants grow 1.5 tons/ha under traditional management but using fertilizer and certified seeds.

Another exceptional PC is *Rarre-Chilalo* in the Hararghe region. This PC is situated in the vicinity of the Alemaya Agricultural University. It was established in 1979 by five members with a capital of ETB 900. In 1986 it had grown to 327 members with a capital of ETB 1.5 million. The annual income of members ranged between ETB 3,700 and ETB 4,500, a very high figure. Rarre-Chilalo owns 3 tractors and 3 trucks and has installed piped water supply and a medical clinic in the PC village. It benefits from scientific agricultural advice given by the staff from the agricultural university. The most profitable enterprise is irrigated production of horticultural crops, the bulk of which is exported by rail to Djibouti. This explains the high income of members.

There are several other highly successful PCs in Ethiopia. Most of them have engaged in some specialized economic activity such as the two mentioned above. They have access to urban markets and they have strong leaders who have been successful in securing favours from the state. It is to cooperatives such as these that both politicians and civil servants, peasants from remote areas and international donors, are guided to be shown the progress of Ethiopian socialism.

But the great majority of the PCs in Ethiopia in 1986/87 were concentrating on subsistence production of cereals under rainfed conditions. Their performance shows a different pattern.

Available data point in the same direction; cereal yields per hectare on collective and individual farms do not differ much. In high potential areas yields approximate 2.0 tons/ha while in subsistence areas they stay at around 1.0 tons/ha[27].

A review of PCs and individual farmers was conducted in Arsi and Bale regions in 1985 as part of the preparation for future Swedish support to agricultural development in those regions[28]. In the review, crop budgets of eight PCs and eight individual household farms in the vicinity of the PCs were compared. The survey concluded the following. The individual household producers make more efficient use of the scarce agricultural resources available to them than do the PCs with the resources at their disposal. In addition to producing more efficiently and using their land more intensively, the household producers market a greater share of their produce - often more than 50%. In the review it was argued that the total surplus available to society from the household based peasant sector is greater than the contribution of an equal number of PC members. The collective organization of peasant production as it functioned in Arsi and Bale in 1985 was not able to realize economies of scale. Neither did PC members receive higher incomes from grain production than household producers did.

Case studies in Gojjam and Wollo have arrived at similar conclusions[29].

In 1986/87 a crop sampling survey was conducted in Arsi including 9,000 samples. Preliminary results show that yields of wheat and barley averaged 18-20 quintals per hectare. There was no statistically significant difference between samples from individual and collective farms although three fourths of the PC farms utilized improved seeds and fertilizer while only one third of the individual farms did so[30].

Records of animal husbandry show a similar picture. PC dairy farms, which keep crossbred cattle, have an average milk yield of 1,000 litres/cow/year in the Arsi region while individual farmers keeping cross-bred cattle produce an average of 1,600 litres/cow/year. The difference is due to management standards[31].

The data referred to above are far from comprehensive. The lack of data can partly be explained by the sensitive nature of investigations comparing yields between individual and collective peasant farms. Nevertheless, a tentative conclusion to be drawn is that PCs in their present stage do not represent a "higher form of production" as compared to the traditional household-based Ethiopian peasant agriculture. Instead, the PCs are less efficient resource users than traditional farmers, when one considers all the external support given to them and their exploitative power vz. neighbouring individual farmers. This is also the spontaneous conclusion given by MOA field staff who work daily with peasants. They often complain of having to work continuously with PCs which show few signs of dynamism, while individual peasant households who are asking for agricultural innovations are being neglected.

Should one, then, conclude that Ethiopia is yet another case where collective farming has failed? Such a conclusion would be premature. PCs may have untapped productive potential.

The official support given to PCs is more ideological and organizational than agronomic/technical. PC members are taught how to set up various committees for a multitude of purposes, how to calculate work points, how to keep records. The MOA field staff even prepares a cropping calendar for them. This is good, but not sufficient. What PCs need in order to become viable production unitsis advice on new technology and land use practices. The big PCs, those with a hundred or more members and equally many hectares of arable land, could benefit from selective mechanization, labour specialization, food processing, multiple land use etc.

MOA has not prepared technical support packages specifically designed for PCs[32]. They occasionally receive tractors and other heavy machinery, but lacking maintenance support, these soon break down. The PC members themselves have not yet proven to be agricultural innovators. The cooperatives use the same methods as they did when their members were individual peasants. A common sight in PC areas during soil preparation time is scores of peasants criss-crossing a large field, everyone with his pair of oxen plodding in different directions without any perceivable coordination. Planting, weeding and harvesting operations also proceed in the same manner as on individual farmers' fields. PC members thus work alongside each other, but they do not take advantage of the economies of scale they implicitly are involved in. This fundamental fact should be a high priority for research and development, if the purpose is to make PCs productive rather than making them just receivers of government handouts and petty exploiters of individual farmers.

The case for rationalization and mechanization in a way adapted to Ethiopian realities - and not just an unimaginative copy of East German realities - is especially obvious on the flat highland plateaux.

Rather than condemning collective peasant production with reference to the mediocre performance of PCs so far, it may be argued that if the ideological agitation and administrative pressure would be de-emphasized in favour of imaginative agronomic, technical and economic experimentation, collective production might have a chance to become rational on technical grounds.

It is quite another thing, though, whether the peasants would think so. One technical argument in favour of collectivization/mechanization is the fragmentation of peasant plots which is considered a hindrance to rational land management. Recent research has shown that peasant associations have their own strategies for coping with future demands for land caused by population increase. In a survey of 17 PAs in the Arsi region using aerial photographs and maps together with field visits, it was shown that land shortage was less pressing than peasant reports to MOA[33] indicate. All PAs had spare land which could be used to accommodate new families. Arsi may be a special case though. In regions such as Gojjam there is an absolute shortage of land.

Cooperative take-off in Arsi?

The high altitude plains of the Arsi region hold great promise for cereal production. The authorities keep a close eye on Arsi, which has always been in the forefront when it comes to implementation of the official development strategy. Officials sometimes jokingly say that "Lenin likes Arsi". The regional MOA office is well equipped and staffed, mainly due to long term Swedish assistance to agricultural development in the region[34]. The famous CADU-project was situated here and its premises have been converted into the regular MOA office. The peasants have a long experience of subjugation to state power, both feudal and revolutionary. They are, thus, predisposed to obey orders.

As mentioned earlier the officials have set themselves an annual target of 10% increase in PC membership. This is by and large fulfilled. The expansion of PCs in Arsi therefore shows a contrasting picture compared with the rest of the country. In Arsi the proportion has steadily risen and was 16% (40,000) of the region's peasant households in 1987. More than four fifths of the PCs in Arsi had reached the second cooperative stage while the corresponding proportion for the country at large was one third[35].

This remarkable expansion is the result of push and pull factors. It can be assumed that a core of very successful PCs, such as Huruta-Hetosa, have given some substance to the agitation for PC formation in the minds of peasants. The well organized MOA office is in a better position than elsewhere to assist newly formed PCs with organization, advice and subsidies.

Proceeding to the push factors, it is known that there are implicit threats in the agitation too. Collectivization is the official policy. A number of advantages are promised to those who comply. Those who stubbornly refuse can, by implication, be considered to harbour anti-revolutionary attitudes. They must be prepared to face sanctions. There are subtle mechanisms at work which would merit deeper analysis.

Whatever the motive, it is a fact that peasants in the Arsi region have joined PCs in great numbers during the 1980s, thus fulfilling the authorities' quota. The pattern was most noticeable in the Ticho district where 22% of all PA members had joined PCs in 1987. In some sub-districts the percentage exceeded 50%[36]. Responding to the question why this massive move occurred one development agent said that "they /the peasants/ know that joining PCs is the order of the day".

A possible explanation could be the following. The peasants have for years been exposed to agitation in favour of the PCs. They know exactly in which ways the PCs are favoured by the authorities and how individual peasant households are discouraged. The situation for individual households is insecure. They have no security of land tenure. All land belongs to the state and individuals can be dispossessed when the authorities so decide. Cases in point are the creation of new PCs and expansion of the nearby state farms in Arsi. Since the revolution some 80,000 ha of land has been expropriated from peasants (grazing and crop land) in order to create state farms on the plains in Arsi and the nearby region of Bale[37]. Every now and then the state farms expand. Peasants are then evicted and moved to other areas. An explanation could be that peasants now joining PCs, reason along the lines "if you can't beat them, join them". They know that they cannot stand up against the state. If they comply with the official policy, they can at least try to reap the benefits promised by the authorities.

In Arsi the promises given to PCs are not empty. The social infrastructure that has been established in a number of PCs, however rudimentary it may appear to an outside observer, may act as an incentive to apply for membership or to start a new PC. The clinics that have been put up in a PC, even though they are ill equipped and lack skilled staff, represent a promise of health care earlier unheard of among the rural population.

These arguments have their limits, though. Increase in PC membership slowed down in 1986/87 while reports from Arsi in early 1988 indicate that it came to a standstill in 1987/88. There are even rumours of PC members who have given up membership and gone back to household based farming. It is still too early to draw any far reaching conclusions from such indicators.

CONCLUDING REMARKS ON COLLECTIVE AGRICULTURE

The attraction of PCs is the promise of state subsidies rather than a conviction that the PC is an instrument for increased, sustainable productivity. But the prevailing approach to PC formation and development is counter productive. Crop and animal husbandry standards among PCs are not superior to those prevailing among household producers. No innovative technology development programme has been designed for PC needs and preconditions. Official support emphasizes ideology and organization, while Government handouts to PCs and the power of PCs to exploit the neighbouring household cultivators create a false impression of economic viability. The official reasoning is that PCs need much initial support in order to take off economically. MOA field staff tell a different story. Their observation is that there is a tendency among PC members and leadership to develop a parasitic attitude. The more support they get, the more they demand. They are beginning to see their privileged position. An officer who challenges their demands can be accused of sabotaging socialist construction next time a party official visits the PC.

Maybe for the first time in Ethiopian history, a group of peasants have the upper hand in their relations with the lower echelons in the bureaucracy.

A serious inquiry into the production problems and potential of PCs in terms of economic viability cannot take place until the political authorities face facts. The illusion of economic viability of PCs can work only as long as the PCs are a small minority and the state can afford to prop them up economically and organizationally. If peasants follow the example from Ticho and join PCs en masse, then subsidization of the collective form of agricultural production will not longer be possible drawing on Ethiopian government funds alone[38]. Paradoxically, the day peasants would comply with official aspirations in great numbers, would be a moment of truth for the politicians. They would then have to come to grips with the real problems of productivity and sustainability in collective agriculture. MOA is ill prepared for such a task today because it has not given serious consideration to production systems for PCs[39]. If viable extension programmes cannot be forwarded, then only those PCs which already have an economically sound footing will remain collective units. There is reason to believe that they would be a minority. The others would slowly revert back to household based agriculture.

SERVICE COOPERATIVES AS AGENTS IN GRAIN TRADE

During the imperial regime grain for urban markets was secured through the land tenure system. In many parts of Ethiopia peasants had share-cropper status and delivered their obligations in kind to landlords, who sold grain thus collected to traders. Freehold peasants sold directly to traders. Farmgate prices fluctuated tremendously. Peasants and small landlords lacked storage facilities and had to sell within a short time after harvest when prices were low. Later on in the season prices increased and those traders and whole-salers who had storage facilities made substantial profits. The urban markets had a steady supply of food grain and prices were moderate[40].

The revolution destroyed this system. The peasantry were freed from all feudal obligations and landlords were chased away. In the first few post-revolutionary years peasants chose to consume the bulk of their produce while reserves were hidden away "for bad days"[41]. For a while the urban markets were starved of grain and acute shortages occurred in many towns particularly during 1976.

In order to gain control of grain marketing the government decided to develop the Agricultural Marketing Corporation (AMC) to an official grain purchasing agent with increasingly expanding mandate. AMC had been created with World Bank support and its intended function was to stabilize prices. However, it fitted well into the emerging socialist ideology to give AMC a quasi-monopoly position.

As part of the emerging strategy Service Cooperatives were to play the role of AMC counterparts. After some years of preparation and gradual build-up, this policy is now being implemented and has gained momentum in the mid 1980s.

In a 'normal' year in the 1980s some 6.2 - 6.5 million metric tons of agricultural products are estimated to be produced in Ethiopia. Most is food crops consumed by the producing households. Some 800,000 tons (15%) are estimated to enter markets[42]. The bulk of the produce is marketed in small quantities (sometimes only a few kilograms) by the producing households on weekly rural markets. Trade to secondary markets is traditionally carried out by licensed traders moving about with small trucks. Such traders are still operating but they have increasingly been brought under AMC control. Altogether AMC annually appropriates 100,000 - 300,000 tons from peasants.

As part of the promotion of AMC as the dominant buyer of peasants' grain, administrative difficulties have been created for its competitors, the private grain traders and the peasant traders. In 1981 private traders were prohibited from operating in the grain sector in Gojjam. In Arsi, private traders were at the same time obliged to deliver 100% of their purchases to AMC. Such a disincentive together with physical harassment of individual traders by the local police, made most traders close down business[43]. The regulations in Gojjam and Arsi were hailed in mass media as yet another socialist victory. In other regions private traders were obliged to deliver 50% of their purchases to AMC at a fixed price. The remainder could be sold in urban markets.

Peasants do some trading themselves. They transport grain bags on donkeyback and sell it in urban markets. However, peasants are only allowed to sell grain in their home district. Due to the overwhelmingly rural character of Ethiopia the urban population is negligible outside regional and national centres. Therefore, in surplus producing regions the prices are low also in small urban markets. It would be attractive for peasants to take their grain to the nearest regional centre or to Addis Abeba. But this is prohibited and the regional and district boundaries are guarded. Sometimes local authorities make restrictions very tight. As a result peasants can only sell for low prices in the small towns. Such low urban market prices favour the small urban population including the district public servants. This is a clear disincentive for surplus production in those regions which are not yet ravaged by environmental degradation. There are numerous reports about peasants sneaking through the bush at night with horses and donkeys loaded with grain, trying to reach major markets or having a rendezvous with a merchant. If they are caught, confiscation of the grain and imprisonment awaits them[44].

In the 1980s Service Cooperatives have been actively encouraged by Government to expand their marketing function in order to become counterparts of AMC. The idea is that peasants should sell all their surplus to their SC, which would act as middleman for AMC. MOA gives advice on book-keeping, accounting and storage operations to SC leaders and employees. The margin of ETB 3-5 per quintal which SCs receive when operating as middlemen for AMC are not distributed to members individually but used for common services and investments.

This system would never work if peasants had the freedom to choose marketing channels on their own. Most years prices at urban markets are higher than those offered by AMC. The authorities have therefore devised a quota system which applies to all peasant producers.

The quota system

The quota system was introduced in 1979 as part of AMC grain procurement guide-lines. It is in principle applicable throughout the cereal producing areas. In actual practise its application varies. The following description refers to the situation in high potential areas[45].

The quota system means essentially that each peasant household has to deliver a fixed amount of grain (specified in commodities) to AMC at a fixed price. The system has advantages to AMC customers - public institutions, urban dwellers associations and the army - which are guarantied a certain supply. It also facilitates AMC planning of purchases. To the peasant producers, the quota system means that they know they will be able to sell a certain amount of grain at a fixed price.

Quotas are set by a national committee composed of representatives of the Ministry of Domestic Trade, AMC and MOA. The basis for determination of the annual nation wide quota is as follows. An estimation of the total cultivated area is computed and multiplied by the estimated average yield per hectare. From this gross production the estimated consumption requirement of producing households, seed requirements and storage losses are deducted. The remainder is, in theory, to be delivered to AMC and to private merchants in regions where these are allowed to operate under license.

The nationwide quota so computed is then divided among regions. Surplus producing regions such as Arsi, Gojjam, Shoa and parts of Gondar are given proportionally high quotas whereas less endowed regions are given lower quotas. Commodity specifications are also given. For example, Gojjam which is a teff region, must deliver most of the quota in this cereal.

Break-down of the regional quota at district, sub-district and finally PA levels is made by committees at these levels including representatives of AMC, MOA, local administrators and PA leaders. Once a PA knows its quota, it is distributed among peasant households. Allocation between households is made by the executive committee. Members are classified as small peasants (<1ha), middle peasants (1-2 ha) and "better-off" peasants (>2 ha). Quotas are then given to households in accordance with their status which is supposed to reflect production capacity.

There is a pressure on peasants to fulfil their quota. Defaulters will be barred from buying necessities at the SC shop, they will not get fertilizer or certified seed etc. In addition, various kinds of informal harassment can be exercised. Threats of imprisonment in the PA jail are not uncommon. The PA leadership is under pressure from the sub-district administration. If the PA does not deliver its quota the whole PA may be barred from buying fertilizer during next season. The formal and informal pressures brought to bear on prospective defaulters varies from area to area and are a matter of local politics.

The quota system appears to be comparatively successful from an administrative point of view. According to senior AMC officials some 60-80% of the computed quota is actually collected annually, except in drought years. Numerous cases have been reported where households have had to sell a goat or sheep in order to buy grain on the local market and thus add up to their own deficient "surplus" production.

The quotas differ greatly. "Better-off" peasants in some parts of Gojjam deliver up to 1.2 ton while their colleagues in Arsi deliver 0.7 ton. In parts of the Wollo region the quota may be set at 0.1 ton per household or even less.

Peasants have complaints about the AMC and the quotas. It is often heard that peasants consider AMC prices too low relative to prices prevailing in the open markets. During the drought 1984/85, enormous price differences were caused by the general shortage of grain which made open market prices sky-rocket. In 1986/87, after a good crop, price differences were much lower, sometimes only a few ETB per quintal.

Peasants usually compare the farm gate price for grain with prices on consumer goods to be bought at SC shops. Although SC shop prices are generally lower than those of private shops in small towns, consumer prices have increased considerably since the revolution while AMC grain prices have been raised only marginally. Terms of trade for peasant household economies thus deteriorated[46].

AMC payments to peasants may be delayed. When peasants deliver their quota to the SC store they get a receipt. AMC pays the SC when they come to pick up the grain. Due to shortage of trucks AMC may come late in the season. The grain, which often is stored on the open ground, may be damaged, and AMC will not pay for that part. AMC may sometimes not come at all to remote areas due to logistical problems. The SC is however not allowed to sell the collected grain to anyone else.

A more general complaint is that those households which happen to have additional amounts of grain for sale after fulfilling their quota have no attractive market outlets due to the quasi-monopoly position of AMC.

AMC has a nationwide grain collection and distribution network. There were in 1986 altogether 1,768 grain collection points, more than 3,000 employees and 170 trucks. The storage capacity of the corporation was 570,000 metric tons in 1986 of which three quarters were concentrated to Arsi, Shoa and Gojjam as well as the terminal market of Addis Abeba. AMC's own transport fleet can only move some 30% of the annual grain procured[47]. AMC must therefore rely heavily on hired trucks as well as cooperation with private merchants, now acting as its agents under strict control.

To achieve total state control of grain marketing would be expensive. AMC's truck fleet, storage facilities and total manpower would have to be vastly increased. There are not enough domestic funds to embark on such a scheme. Therefore it is understood that the AMC monopoly would be built up gradually. In the meantime private merchants will have to be tolerated. In AMC's plans for the future there will be one branch office in every one of the 577 sub-districts. Grain collection points would be reduced to a manageable number and located close to major roads so as to facilitate transportation. Coordination with the Ethiopian Domestic Distribution Corporation (EDDC) would be effected[48].

CONCLUDING REMARKS

Coming back to Göran Hydén's hypothesis, this analysis of collective agriculture and grain marketing has shown how the peasantry is captured by the state. For historical reasons, the Ethiopian state has a higher administrative capacity than its southern neighbours. Ethiopian peasants were integrated in the feudal system prevailing before the revolution. In the early days of revolution and land reform, peasants took advantage of the chaos created by internal strife and external aggression. They tried to escape into a self-contained life within their own communities. A visible evidence of this was the reluctance of peasants to sell grain to urban markets mentioned earlier. The military government realized the danger to the urban and public sectors of an un-captured peasantry hiding away their potential marketable surplus. Determined efforts to knit together the peasant economy with the public sector were therefore made. Utilizing a socialist planning ideology, the government seizes the peasantry with military resoluteness and administrative efficiency. Villages, cooperatives, marketing and pricing policy all aim at controlling the production and circulation of rural commodities. This is summarized in the slogan "socialization of the means of production and distribution", which is flagged everywhere.

The administrative network is tightening around the peasantry in order to secure a certain amount of grain for the public sector. It is not necessarily a surplus that is being extracted. AMC demands quotas also from peasants eking out a meagre subsistence.

The system functions moderately well for the purpose of appropriating a tribute from the peasantry to be consumed by the public sector including the armed forces. But it can be questioned whether the system is capable of achieving capital accumulation on a national scale.

The instruments used to capture the peasantry are of an administrative nature with built-in coercive mechanisms and they often have a demoralizing effect on the producers. People are not stimulated to be innovative. Work output is not linked to individual benefits. Such thoughts are anathema to the official ideology. Over and over people are told by officials that it is their national obligation to work harder, that the fruits of their labour will be used to strengthen socialism. They know that in actual practise this means that they themselves will not get the benefits.

It appears that the political strategists at the highest level value tight control of a stagnant production higher than the alternative - to loosen control and accept capitalist tendencies within the peasantry together with increased productivity among at least the emerging entrepreneurial peasants.

With an annual population growth of 2.9% and recurrent crop failures in the northern and eastern parts of the country, it would be a necessity to get peasant agriculture moving in the high potential areas. Policy modifications which increase the role of individual incentives and allow for flexibility in production, pricing and marketing may then have to be introduced. This insight is well established at the level of senior civil servants in the ministries. But it remains to convince the real powerholders: the inner circle of the politbureau in the Workers Party, where attitudes are doctrinaire. The leading politicians are far removed from the realities of peasant agriculture and no one dares tell them about the shortcomings of the socialist reforms. The political prestige invested in the socialist reforms is significant, so they are likely to turn a deaf ear to criticism.

Whatever political advantage the leaders see in state interventionist agricultural policies, they may eventually have to face the fact that these policies are failures in terms of growth of productivity. Then it will be realized that more than a decade has been lost in the race between agricultural development and population increase.

NOTES

1. The first comprehensive monograph analysing peasant response to drought and food shortages is Dessalegn Rahmato, *Famine and Survival Strategies. A Case Study from Northeast Ethiopia* (Institute of Development Studies, Food and Famine Monograph Series No. 1, 1988).

2. Ministry of Domestic Trade, *A Short Note on Current Grain Marketing and Price Policy* (Addis Abeba, 1986).

3. In addition to the periodic droughts which threaten millions with starvation, there is a structural imbalance emerging in food production/consumption needs. The World Bank estimates that 14.7 million Ethiopians are "food insecure", i.e. suffer from a continuously inadequate diet caused by persistent inability to acquire food by whatever means - producing, buying etc. See World Bank, *Report of the Task Force on Food Security in Africa* (1988). USAID estimates that the five year average production 1979/80 - 1983/84 was 6.2 million metric tons of grain equivalent which suggests a deficit of 350,000 metric tons in a 'normal' year. If production does not show a clear upward trend in the late 1980's, this would leave a net deficit of 2 million tons to be covered by import in 1990. See USAID/ADDIS, *An Appraisal of Ethiopia's Agricultural Prospects* (1986).

4. The concerned donors include Sweden, Italy, Canada, The World Bank, EEC and the African Development Bank. On the Ethiopian side the spokesmen are the Ministry of Agriculture, The Ministry of Domestic Trade and the Office of the National Commission for Central Planning. The exchange of views takes place during field missions, annual sector reviews, consultations and negotiations. While discussion can be frank and heated during meetings, the Agreed Minutes and other documents are often watered down to reflect a common consensus, i.e. the need to increase production. My personal experience is that the Ethiopian administrators have a thorough appreciation of donor points of view, but they cannot communicate criticism of the collectivized agricultural sector to their political superiors which view agriculture in very ideological terms.

5. Cohen, J.M. and Isaksson, N.I. (1988) "Food Production Strategy Debates in Revolutionary Ethiopia", in *World Development* Vol. XVI, No. 3.

6. Hyden, G. (1983) *No Shortcuts to Progress. African Development in Perspective*. Heinemann, London.

7. Quoted in Levine, D. (1974) *Greater Ethiopia. The Evolution of a Multiethnic Society*. The University of Chicago Press.

84

8. The regional administration was reorganized in late 1987 in connection with the establishment of the People's Democratic Republic of Ethiopia. Since the material for the present analysis was collected in 1984-87, references will be made to the old administrative set-up including 14 regions, 102 districts (awraja) and close to 600 sub-districts (woreda).

9. The empirical basis of my argumentation is partly drawn from "grey" material such as office memoranda, letters, notes-for-the-file, project proposals available in Addis Abeba and partly from personal experience and field observations. During 1984-87 I served as administrator of SIDA's support to agriculture, forestry and soil conservation in Ethiopia. During numerous field trips I had the opportunity of visiting MOA regional offices, cooperatives and peasant associations and to hold lengthy discussions with officials, technical experts and peasants. The primary sources of this paper are thus my own notebooks.

10. Peasant Associations, Producers' and Service Cooperatives are usually treated together in the literature. Some references are given below. Empirical studies include Adelstål, B. (1985) *A Training Programme for Agricultural Service Cooperatives in Ethiopia*. Addis Abeba.; Dejene, A. (1987) *Peasants, Agrarian Socialism and Rural Development in Ethiopia*. Westview Press.; Abate, A. (1983) "Peasant Associations and Collective Agriculture in Ethiopia: Promise and Performance", in *Journal of African Studies*, Vol. X. No. 3.; Rahmato, D. (1984) *Agrarian Reform in Ethiopia*. Scandinavian Institute of African Studies, Uppsala.; Woube, M. (1986) *Problems of Land Reform Implementation in Rural Ethiopia. A Case Study of Dejen and Wolmera District*. Kulturgeografiska Institutionen, Uppsala.; Poluha, E. (1988) *Central Planning and Local Reality. A Case Study of Producers Cooperatives in Ethiopia*. Studies in Social Anthropology, forthcoming, Stockholm.; Ståhl, M. (1977) *New Seeds in Old Soil. A Study of the Land Reform Process in Western Wollega 1975-76*. Scandinavian Institute of African Studies, Uppsala. Reviews and general analysis are found in; Lirenso, A. (1983) "State Policies in Production, Marketing and Pricing of Food Grains: The Case of Ethiopia" in *Africa Development* Vol. VIII, No. 1.; Lirenso, A. (1985) "Rural Service Cooperatives in Ethiopia: Tasks and Performance". in *Northeast African Studies*, Vol. VIII, No 3.; Abate, A. and Kiros, F.G. (1980) *Land Reform, Structural Changes and Rural Development in Ethiopia*. Institute of Development Studies. Discussion Paper No. 6.; Kiros, F.G. "Mobilizing the Peasantry for Rural Development: the Ethiopian Experiment in Progress", in Rubenson S. (1984) (ed.) *Proceedings of the Seventh International Conference of Ethiopian Studies*. Scandinavian Institute of African Studies, Uppsala.; Genberg, B., Sthål, M. and Taube, E. (1982) *Report on Peasant Associations and Agricultural Cooperatives in Ethiopia*. Addis Abeba.; Yadeta, G. (1987) "Some Aspects of Cooperatives vis-a-vis the State in Ethiopia" in *Social Change. Journal of the Council for Social Development*, Vol. 17, No. 2.; Harbeson, J. "Socialist Policies in Ethiopia" in Rosberg, C. (1979)

(ed.) *African Socialism*. Berkeley Institute for International Studies.; Hareide, D. (1986) *Peasant Associations as Agents for Development*. UN Office for Emergency Operations in Ethiopia.; ILO (1983) *Agrarian Transformation. The Case of Ethiopia*. Workshop on Transformation of Agrarian Systems in Centrally Planned Economies of Africa, Arusha, Tanzania. For a review by a Soviet scholar see Galperin, G. (1981) "Stages of Agrarian Revolution", in *Asia and Africa Today*, No. 6. The only comprehensive description and analysis of villagization so far is Cohen, J.M. and Isaksson, N.I. (1987) *Villagization in the Arsi Region of Ethiopia*. Swedish University of Agricultural Sciences, Rural Development Studies No. 19. The impact of villagization on women is analyzed in Alopaeus-Ståhl, D. (1987) *The Women's Dimension in the Villagization Process in Arsi*. Swedish Embassy, Addis Abeba.

11. An illustrative episode occurred when a team of consultants from the Swedish Cooperative Centre visited the AEPA headquarters in 1982 and brought up the question how AEPA could further the interest of its members by influencing the Ministry of Domestic Trade to raise farm gate prices. The AEPA officials then plainly explained that in this particular case it was their revolutionary duty to first and foremost guard the interests of the urban proletariat i.e. to make sure that food prices were kept at a low level.

12. Information from MOA, zonal office of South Eastern Agricultural Development Zone, Asella.

13. The *Villagization Guide-lines* (in Amharic) are presented in Cohen and Isaksson (1987), *op.cit.*

14. A useful summary together with rich references related to agrarian issues at the end of Haile Selassie's rule is given in Cohen, J.M., Goldsmith, A.A. and Mellor, J.W. (1976) *Revolution and Land Reform in Ethiopia; Peasant Associations, Local Government and Rural Development*. Cornell University Rural Development Committee. Occasional Papers No. 6.

15. *Proclamation No. 31/1975* (Public Ownership of Rural Lands) and *Proclamation No. 71/1975* (Peasant Associations).

16. Accounts of the early communal farms are given in Abate, *op.cit.*, Poluha, *op.cit,*; Ståhl, *op.cit.*

17. The directive is not officially translated to English. Its content is summarized in Kiros (1984), *op.cit.*

18. The East German adviser to MOA, Rainer Falch, has summarized his experiences of PC organization and performance in Falch, R. (1982) *Some Questions Concerning the Development of Agricultural Producers' and Service*

Cooperative Societies as well as Settlement Sites in Socialist Ethiopia, Final Report of the Main Results of Advisory Activities. Addis Abeba.

19. The first villages to be established in Ethiopia date back to the 1970s, when the highland population in Bale region was villagized by authorities in the aftermath of the Somali invasion in that region. At the same time villages were established in the Wabe area of the Arsi region to settle peasants who had been evicted to give room for state farms. Research on the Wabe villages is underway by Ingvar Jonsson. A brief note on the formation of Wabe-villages is given in SIDA, *Proposal for SIDA Support to Rural Development in Arsi and Bale 1986/87 - 1988/89*. Annex 14 (1985). See also Cohen and Isaksson, (1987), *op.cit.*

20. The description is based on material I collected during visits to the Shoa, Gojjam and Arsi regions in 1981. The material consists of official records and notes from discussions with MOA and local administration officials as well as PA and PC leaders. For a summary see Genberg, Ståhl and Taube, *op.cit.*

21. I witnessed a drastic illustration of the contradiction between PC members and individual peasants in the remote town of Mertule Mariam in Gojjam in May 1986. When the local peasants heard that the area around the town would be villagized they complained to the district administration. The peasants raised the issues of high compulsory grain quotas, collectivization of production and villagization. They objected to all these policies. When the administration refused to take their complaints seriously, trouble started. The peasants mobilized a force of several hundred armed men who marched against Mertule Mariam. They tried to destroy a bridge in order to block communication. The administration managed to get in touch with the administrative headquarters in Bahr Dar from which army units - helicopter gunships - were dispatched. The only rural people who sided with the district administration and the townspeople were PC members from nearby areas. They were also armed and made themselves prepared to fight the approaching peasant army at the outskirts of Mertule Mariam. At this time the army arrived. The helicopters spread havoc among the traditional peasant warriors and the rebellion came to an end. When I arrived to Mertule Mariam a few days later, some fifty peasant warriors had gathered in the administrative compound. They were PC members. All of them got fresh supplies of bullets as a reward for their support to the administration.

22. Eva Poluha gives a detailed account from Gojjam of changing relation between kinfolk and friends including gender issues. Poluha, *op.cit.*

23. Points iv, viii, ix, x, xii and xiii are sensitive. At official meetings between donors and the Ethiopian administration they are dismissed by Ethiopian

officials. Nevertheless, it is well known that they are practised. Point xiii is only implemented in certain districts.

24. Jonsson, I. (1986) "Vad händer på den etiopiska landsbygden?", in *Geografiska notiser*, No 4.

25. PMAC, *Ten Year Perspective Plan.*

26. Ministry of Agriculture, South Eastern Agricultural Development Zone, *Annual Report 1986/87* (SEAD Publication No. 6, 1987).

27. These figures show that there is an untapped potential in peasant agriculture. Given improved husbandry and inputs a peasant farm can yield close to 3 tons/ha according to MOA field trials.

28. SIDA, *op.cit.* When the results of this review were to be discussed in the MOA, the mission leader was informed that the Minister had no intention of entertaining a report which contained criticism against collective peasant agriculture. Consequently no discussion took place. SIDA studied the report and drew the conclusion that it was not worthwhile funding peasant agriculture in Arsi and Bale under the prevailing political circumstances, because the great majority of the peasants - non-PC households - did not benefit from MOA activities. SIDA support to rural development in Arsi and Bale was subsequently directed to 'policy-neutral' activities such as water supply, soil conservation and road maintenance. In 1988 the Swedish government informed the Ethiopian government of its intention to withdraw completely from funding rural development in Arsi and Bale when the agreement expires in 1989.

29. Poluha, *op.cit.*; Rahmato (1987), *op.cit.*

30. The crop sampling study was undertaken in November 1986 - January 1987. Data were processed and analyzed in 1987-88. The results will be published in early 1989 by MOA, South Eastern Agricultural Development Zone.

31. Information from the zonal office of MOA - South Eastern Agricultural Development Zone.

32. The challenge to research has been formulated thus: "The introduction of PCs, sometimes cultivating units of over 250 ha, presents a completely new challenge to research workers. Large units provide an opportunity to introduce cultural methods of weed control and crop and pasture rotation and to avoid excessive dependence on agricultural chemicals. Major opportunities exist for introducing truly mixed farming incorporating improved animal husbandry practices. The major research challenge presented by PCs is the improvement of yield levels, the maintenance of farm employment, and the minimizing of

foreign exchange costs". This challenge was not, however, systematically explored by MOA. See Adams, M.E. (1985) "Assessment of ARDU's Extension Service", in *Review of ARDU*, SIDA.

33. Cohen, J.M. and Jonsson, I. (1987) "Size of Peasant Association Holdings and Government Policies: Questions Raised by Recent Research in Ethiopia's Arsi Region" *Northeast African Studies*, Vol. IX, No. 1.

34. A comprehensive analysis of the CADU/ARDU project during the period 1967-84 is provided in Cohen, J.M. (1987) *Integrated Rural Development. The Ethiopian Experience and the Debate*. Scandinavian Institute of African Studies, Uppsala.

35. SEAD, *op.cit.*

36. *Ibid.*

37. Ministry of State Farms (1986) *Towards a Strategy for the Development of State Farms in Ethiopia, Vol. I*. Addis Abeba.

38. Funds for investment in agricultural development come traditionally from the World Bank and SIDA. Recently EEC and the African Development Bank have become donors. Fresh funds in large quantities have been slow in materializing during the 1980's. MOA and the donors have discussed a development package called PADEP (Peasant Agricultural Development Programme) emphasizing the conventional seed/fertilizer package combined with decentralization of MOA offices, focus on agro-ecological diversification, intensified extension, training programmes for staff and peasants and efficient marketing. Detailed project preparation reports have been written. Among them are World Bank reports on Shoa, on Gondar and Gojjam and on Wollega, Kefa & Illubabor. SIDA prepared an earlier report on Gojjam and Gondar in 1983, while the document SIDA, 1985, on Arsi and Bale was prepared within the context of PA-DEP. Consultations and negotiations move slowly, the stumbling block being controversy over pricing/marketing and collectivization. An overview of the arguments is given in Cohen and Isaksson, (1988), *op.cit.*

39. This should not necessarily be interpreted as a lack of interest within MOA for technical innovations. The ministry has been absorbed in repeated reorganizations which have consumed most of its energy during the 1980's. Moreover, due to the lack of development funds there have not been resources for biological and technical research, development and extension.

40. Holmberg, J. (1977) *Grain Marketing and Land Reform in Ethiopia*. Scandinavian Institute of African Studies, Uppsala.

41. For a case study from Wollega 1976 see Ståhl, *op.cit.*

42. Ministry of Domestic Trade, *op.cit.*; Cohen and Isaksson (1987) *op.cit.*

43. Toborn, J. (1985) *Marketing and Distribution in Ethiopia*. SIDA/ARDU.

44. *Ibid,* I have personally been witness to a case in Gojjam in 1986, where eight peasants were put in jail for having tried to market their grain outside their home district.

45. The information on quotas has been gathered through interviews with officials of AMC and MOA.

46. Rahmato, D. (1987) *op.cit.* quotes AMC figures showing how terms of trade have deteriorated for peasants in Wollo. According to these figures consumer goods prices during the period 1978-82 had increased as follows: shoes - 174%, cloth - 140%, sugar - 157% and fertilizer - 177%.

47. Ministry of Domestic Trade *op.cit.*

48. *Ibid.* One can speculate if the purpose of such a coordination would be to make delivery of consumer goods to SC shops conditional on fulfilment of the grain quota.

CHAPTER 3

STATE, COOPERATIVES AND DEVELOPMENT: EGYPT 1908-1988.

by Hans Holmén.

INTRODUCTION.

Literature discussing cooperation in the Third World has often assumed that
cooperation - due to the universal strength of the cooperative principles - owns
an ability to act as an autonomous force upon a country's development. Thus, it
has been assumed not only that cooperatives will raise agricultural production
in general, but also that they will "solve the problem of food supply in the Third
World" (Bonow 1969). Particularly, cooperatives have been expected to improve
the situation of the poor (Young et al 1981). Further, cooperatives have been
expected to foster a democratic spirit - "Shule der Fundamentaldemokrati-
sierung" - in allegedly non-democratic developing nations (Klöwer 1977). The
idea of cooperation, it has generally been assumed, must therefore be
introduced from outside and specialists and public officials are given the
mission to develop a cooperative "awareness" among potential peasant-
members. This also explains why, in the Middle East, little use has been made
of traditional and indigenous forms for mutual aid when rural cooperatives have
been established (von Muralt 1969). The "fairness" of the cooperative principles
has also led to the assumption that they will promote egalitarianism and
eliminate class-distinctions among members (UNRISD 1975).

At the same time as cooperatives are seen as agents of change, they have been
seen as a guarantee for the preservation of "Gemeinschaft" in emerging new
societies (Hirschfeld 1978). While on the one hand being innovations in their
local environment and on the other hand presupposing members' active
participation and democratic rule, cooperatives would thus provide a cushion to
development and the social and cultural uprooting that inevitably goes with it.
For reasons like these, the conclusion has often been drawn that cooperatives
represent "the most valid of the solutions for the Third World and its problems"
(Konopnicki 1978) and that, "theoretically and in the long run", cooperatives will
"resolve most if not all problems of development" (ICA 1978). Only recently has
it been underlined that the impact of cooperatives on development - and the
niches open for "true" cooperative enterprise - generally is rather limited (see
e.g. Hanel 1985; Münkner 1983). Obviously, much cooperative literature has
been filled with "unrealistic expectations" (Dülfer 1975).

It needs to be stressed that no "universal principle" of organization, and no particular "ethos" is likely to possess such an ability to act as an autonomous force in a development process. "Ethos" and principles of organization do not constitute independent variables which act freely upon society. Rather, they are shaped in concrete historical situations - by people - with different needs, resources, world-views, power positions and interests. The roles, structures, functions and performance of cooperatives are thus not primarily to be sought in a set of "universally acknowledged" cooperative principles. In practical life they rather tend to be determined by the specific situations in which cooperatives operate and are also likely to reflect the overall development of - and power-struggles within - their areas of operation.

As a rule, Third World rural cooperatives have not been permitted to evolve from below. Instead they have, in most cases, been established by national governments assisted by foreign or international cooperative "experts". On many occasions young and inexperienced governments in developing nations (often populist and easily militarized regimes) have suddenly found themselves in control of a large state apparatus, that has either been taken over from or handed over by the former colonial power. A problem arises when such governments, in the name of modernization, organize the peasantry in supervised cooperatives at the same time as their most urgent need is to consolidate power and establish political legitimacy, to gain control over economy and national territory, (Clapham 1985). In such circumstances there is generally little room for the voluntary and participatory aspects of cooperation.

For cooperatives to successfully function as agents of change and instruments of development, let alone as democratic organizations, a basic precondition is obviously that they are permitted to function as self-help organizations, i.e. be established as a response to a felt need, without undue control from local or central authorities. Moreover, as cooperatives do not operate in a vacuum, their overall political and economic environment must be one that permits all kinds of autonomous organization in interest groups of which cooperative societies, labour unions and political parties are only a few examples. But even then, cooperatives can only (directly) benefit those who have a stake in cooperative membership. For other groups, I can not see how a "cooperative ethos" could be "developed".

AIM AND SCOPE.

Agricultural cooperatives have existed in Egypt during the last 80 years and they have seen the coming and going of highly diverging governments. The purpose of this paper is to illuminate - in the perspective of Egypt's overall development and shifting development strategies - the varying roles assigned to agricultural cooperatives. A further purpose is to discuss the effect on cooperative "ethos" that is the outcome of Egypt's ambition to utilize supervised agricultural cooperatives as a major instrument for planned rural development.

COOPERATION, DECOLONIZATION AND STRATIFICATION, 1900-1950.

The first attempts to build cooperative societies in Egypt were made already in the first years of the 20th century. Egypt at that time was under direct foreign domination and the British colonial power had managed to turn the country into one "large mono-crop economy" (Abdussallam & Abusedra 1985), specialized in cultivation of cotton as raw material for the Lancashire textile industry (Castle 1976). Around 80% of the population lived in rural areas and were directly dependent on agriculture for their living. Private land titles had been introduced in the 19th century, but due to the extreme scarcity of arable land in the Nile valley and delta (96% of Egypt is desert), Muslim inheritance law which divides property among a great number of heirs, lack of organized credit for small landowners, and generous grants of land to the king's favourites and members of the royal family, a very unequal pattern of landownership had evolved. Economically and politically Egypt was dominated by a small but powerful class of large landowners while the majority of the population consisted of a mass of impoverished smallholders and landless labourers. In the late 19th century, 1% of the landowners owned 40% of the arable land while, at the other extreme, 80% of the landowners owned only 20% of the land (Richards 1982). All official credit was geared towards cotton cultivation, particularly through the Egyptian Agricultural Bank, one of the largest foreign companies in Egypt at the time. Small peasants had to rely on private usurers which, sooner or later, would force them to join the ranks of the landless proletariat.

In the first decade of the 20th century, the nationalist movement, in order to ameliorate the exploitation of the small peasants - in opposition to both the colonial power and the indigenous government - tried to establish cooperative societies as a means to fill a gap in the credit-system (el- Haydary 1983; Treydte 1971). Generally, the "birth" of the cooperative movement in Egypt is attributed to the activities of the 'private philantropist' Omar Lotfy who had studied cooperation in Italy under Luigi Luzatti. Lotfy was also a 'distinguished' member of the National Party which wanted the proposed cooperatives to act not only in an economic capacity but also as political organizations (Moharram 1983a), constituting the prerequisites for political independence (Radwan 1977).

While political power, trade, and financial markets were in the hands of foreigners (for example, the banks were British-owned and unofficial usurers of Greek origin (Richards 1982) controlled most uninstitutionalized agricultural credit), land, emerging industries and local power institutions were largely

Map 1. The Nile Valley

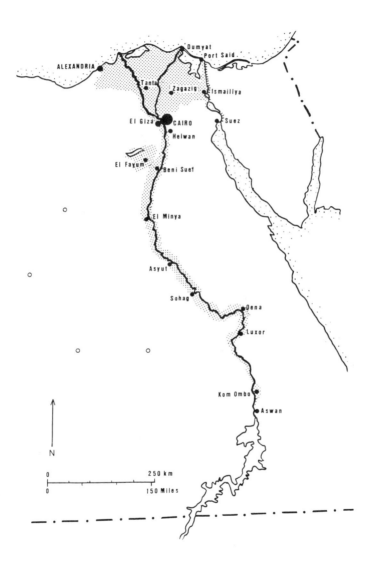

Egypt covers an area of ca. 1 million km^2 but the inhabited and cultivated Nile Valley accounts for only 4% of the national territory, the rest being desert.

controlled by a dependent class of absentee latifundists of Turkish (i.e. Ottoman) origin. Thus, although ethnically heterogeneous, the whole political and economic elite in the country was more or less alien to its population. Capital formation by means of cooperative enterprise and strengthening the economic bargaining power of the peasantry was, thus, a highly political matter - even when political motivations were not openly aired - and even if it would only benefit a small, non-radical, but indigenous rural middle-class. It was only natural then that neither the British nor the Egyptian government favoured the cooperative idea and, from the onset, tried to suppress the movement (Moharram 1983a). However, their attitudes changed somewhat after the economic crisis of 1907 when the British-owned Egyptian Agricultural Bank suffered great losses due to the peasants' inability to repay loans. Lord Kitchener, the de-facto ruler of Egypt, then asked civil servants to encourage farmers to form cooperative societies, while the Egyptian government remained rather negative to the idea. Omar Lotfy succeeded in establishing the first agricultural cooperative in 1908, and in 1909 the first cooperative society for trade and manufacture was created. As there was no cooperative legislation, these societies were registered as 'credit unions' under the Corporation Law (ibid).

The spread of cooperatives was facilitated by unexpected effects of a law that was promulgated to protect small peasants from having their land confiscated by financial institutes. The Five Feddan Law of 1912, intended to prevent the seizure for debts of holdings less than five feddan[1] in size, had the adverse effect of excluding the majority of peasants from institutionalized credit and reduced the lending of the Egyptian Agricultural Bank with the result that by 1913 the bank's loans offered to small-holders only equaled a quarter of their debts to private money-lenders (Radwan 1977). This seemingly humanitarian law did not prohibit the seizure of land *per se*. It merely gave the indigenous elite, who controlled most of the unofficial credit market, a monopoly on taking land as collateral for loans. Whether this was a victory for the Egyptian upper-class or a deliberate attempt from the colonial power to buy their support can not be determined here. In any case, it greatly enhanced the concentration of land into the hands of a few.

Lack of favourable credit sources helped to provide a breeding ground for cooperatives, but they still faced a harsh environment with continuing government suspiciousness. The cooperative movement grew slowly and between 1908 and 1919 only 11 credit societies and 1870 members were registered (Treydte 1971). Actually, there had been a larger number of societies before the first world war but after the death of Omar Lotfy many had disappeared, especially during the war years.

---

1. One feddan is roughly equal to one acre.

In 1919 Egypt gained formal independence (but the British still stayed as occupants until 1936, and in the Suez canal zone until 1956) and a few years later, in an atmosphere more conducive to national development, the first cooperative legislation was promulgated in 1923. Thereafter, pressure mounted for the formation of agricultural cooperatives in order to cope with the effects of successive economic crises, culminating in the great depression of 1929-32 (Radwan 1977). An exporter of primary commodities like Egypt was hit especially hard by these recessions and the inter-war period was one of "agricultural involution" with per capita production actually declining from the pre-war level (Richards 1982). The new law established that any 10 farmers could form an agricultural cooperative company and a Cooperative Department was created in the Ministry of Agriculture (Baker 1978). However, the law did not permit the full development of cooperatives as self-administrating units (el-Haydary 1983; Treydte 1971) and it did not define the role of the State (Moharram 1983a). But it did fix a share-value just high enough to exclude participation of low-income groups (Baker 1978). The growth of the cooperative movement was hampered by such limitations, but also by frequent changes of ministers, which all were ignorant of cooperation, believing that they represented the first step towards communism (ibid).

In 1927, a second law, more positive to cooperatives and removing most deficiencies of the previous legislation, was enacted and, in 1931, the Crédit Agricole d'Egypte was established with the aim to provide cooperatives with necessary credit at low interest rates. The result was a noticeable expansion of the movement but the government maintained its tight grip over the cooperatives, primarily by limiting the allocation of funds to the Crédit Agricole. Moreover, as the cooperatives were dominated by large landowners, these influential patrons managed to ensure themselves favourable treatment and better terms of credit than could be attained by their poorer fellow members (Richards 1982). Through such preferential treatment, the wealthy landowners managed to concentrate even more land into their own hands but, while the number of cooperative societies increased from 11 to 514 between 1919 and 1930, their economic turnover stagnated (Treydte 1971).

In addition to their primary function as credit suppliers, cooperatives were used by reformers during the inter war years to provide the organizational framework for a social security system throughout the countryside. To this end stipulations were made that part of the profits realized by the societies were to be set aside for social services and in 1939 supervision of cooperatives was shifted to the Ministry of Social Affairs (Baker 1978). In the 1940s, wartime difficulties and overall shortages led to a renewed call for governmental support and the State made use of cooperatives for the distribution of rationed fertilizers and other commodities in short supply. The number of cooperative societies more than doubled between 1942 and 1944 (Treydte 1971) but, due to continued central control and the still limited allocation of funds to the Crédit

Agricole, the ratio of societies dealing with the bank fell from over 50% in 1938 to less than 20% in 1944 (Moharram 1983a).

Agricultural cooperatives in the first half of the 20th century were turned into "clubs for the village notables" (Radwan 1977) and it is noteworthy that while in 1942 a law was enacted that legalized industrial trade unions, it forbade the organization of agricultural workers (Richards 1982) - a reflection of the strong political power of the landed aristocracy in Egypt before 1952. From its emergence as an emancipatory movement, the cooperatives had evolved into apparatuses in the hands of the local and national elites, and Egypt's cooperative system as it evolved during the first half of this century clearly reflected the main features of the prevailing political system, being no more than credit institutions catering for the needs of the dominant class, with little or no regard for the needs of the majority of small agricultural producers.

Socio-economic conditions in Egypt around 1950, particularly in its rural areas, can best be described as catastrophic. Expansion of cultivated areas through land reclamation and extended irrigation-works was unable to keep pace with population growth, which more than doubled in less than 50 years. The number of agriculturally employed had increased four times as fast as the cultivated area. Poverty and underemployment reached enormous levels and malnutrition was widespread. While the vast majority of rural inhabitants was completely landless, and more than 75% of the landowners owned too little land to support a family, sources of income outside agriculture were extremely scarce. For small landowners, fragmentation of holdings increased rapidly. The situation for the medium and large landowners was much better. This is partly explained by their possibilities to sequestrate land from indebted smallholders, but also because they were able to purchase newly reclaimed land which, from time to time, was sold from public domains. This practice largely offset the adverse effects of dividing, through inheritance, the total area owned by these groups (Radwan 1977). By the late 1940s less than 0.5% of the landowners owned 35% of the cultivable area while, at the other extreme, more than 94% of the landowners shared another 35% of the land.

In the late 1940s it was clear that this situation could no longer be maintained. Land reform bills were proposed by some liberal politicians but were decisively rejected by the landlord dominated parliament. It soon became obvious that something more formidable than a tenancy reform was needed. The long awaited overthrow of government came in 1952 when a group of young officers managed to seize power. Already on the day of the coup a Land Reform was announced and it only took six weeks before its implementation was commenced.

REVOLUTION, AGRARIAN REFORM AND COOPERATIVES
AFTER 1952.

The modern system of agricultural cooperatives is inseparably connected to the
successive Agrarian Reforms of the 1950s and 1960s. The most striking feature
of these reforms is that they were not limited to a change in the tenure system
only, but represented a broad attack on Egypt's rural problems within a wider
context of national development planning. Ceilings on landownership were first
put at 300 feddan, later to be reduced to 200 and then to 50 feddan per person
and 100 feddan per family until land redistribution came to a halt in 1969.
Although the redistribution programme affected only 13% of the cultivated
area and 9% of the rural population (Radwan 1977), its socio-political impact
was great as it ended the power of the old landed elite and represented a
genuine attempt to transform the agrarian system of the country. Land
redistribution was supplemented by the establishment of minimum wages for
agricultural labour, improved tenancy regulations, and establishment of
agricultural labour unions.

Beneficiaries of Agrarian Reform were to be allotted land holdings of five
feddan but generally only received plots of about three feddan in size. Receivers
of Agrarian Reform land were obliged to join a new type of cooperative
societies which under government supervision were to replace the old large
landowners in the organization of production, credit supply and marketing of
agricultural produce. Supervision and extension was administered by the
Ministry of Social Affairs and was seen as a temporary phenomenon to be
withdrawn "as soon as the members no longer needed the services of the
supervisor" (Marei 1954). Moreover, the entire Agrarian Reform was conceived
of as part of an even larger, interrelated, development package, including
industrialization and reclamation of desert land. Investments in agriculture were
"of a respectable rate" and the drive to industrialize was not to be financed by a
repressive taxation of agriculture (Baker 1978).

To gain economies of scale in handling inputs and output and to overcome the
serious problem of land fragmentation, land distributed under the Agrarian
Reform laws was pooled into a system of block farming. The peasants remained
owners of the land but in any specific area all redistributed land was
consolidated and divided into three major blocks, each designated for a
specified crop, permitting joint operations in major tasks like plowing and the
picking of cottonleaf worms. Each peasant had a piece of land within each block
permitting him to grow both subsistence and market crops. A local cooperative
manager, *mushrif*, usually an agronomist, was centrally appointed to run the
local society and under his supervision a unified three year crop rotation cycle
was applied. The main effect of this triennial rotation system was that cotton
was now grown every third year. The biennial rotation that particularly small

peasants had previously practiced exhausted land and caused severe soil-damage in areas where cotton was grown. To facilitate the supervision of production the Agrarian Reform cooperatives also provided credit in kind for the desired crops and were given a monopoly on the marketing of strategic products which the peasants delivered according to a quota system.

Figure 1: Cropping Pattern Imposed through Cooperatives.

		Block 1	Block 2	Block 3
Year 1	Winter	Bersim	Bersim	Wheat
	Summer	Maize	Cotton	Rice
Year 2	Winter	Bersim	Wheat	Bersim
	Summer	Cotton	Rice	Maize
Year 3	Winter	Wheat	Bersim	Bersim
	Summer	Rice	Maize	Cotton

This "scientific" system had some immediate advantages. Consolidation saved land and may have increased yields. Cultivation of a single crop in one large area allowed the elimination of the maze of separate paths, mud-walls and canals, and it has been estimated that this increased available acreage by some 10 to 20% (Radwan 1977). Consolidated cropping harmonized irrigation requirements and reduced plant diseases. All in all, the various effects of the consolidated block-farming and crop rotation system was estimated to have increased yields of land by as much as 20% (ibid).

A similar cooperative system was established in Land Reclamation areas outside the Nile valley and delta where land was distributed to landless agricultural labourers, smallholders and demobilized soldiers in plots equal to those in Agrarian reform areas (3-5 feddan per family). Parallel to these systems of supervised Agrarian Reform and Land Reclamation cooperatives the government encouraged, but did not interfere in, the activities of the 'traditional' cooperative societies on land unaffected by Agrarian Reform, so called 'old land'. That is, until 1961, Egypt's new system of agricultural cooperatives was confined to the limited and dispersed Agrarian Reform areas, and to some relatively isolated Land Reclamation areas but in that year cooperative membership was made compulsory and the system was extended to cover the whole country and to include all peasants. For this reason, a third cooperative multi-purpose system was created to oversee agricultural production on 'old lands'. Beside these three multi-purpose cooperative hierarchies were also established nine types of single-purpose cooperative organizations, each collecting and marketing a special product (cotton, flax, rice, potatoes, etc.). Products were delivered in quotas to the local multi-purpose societies which in turn delivered to the specialized societies.

Gross production requirements are centrally determined. After the concerned ministries have settled the national agricultural production plan for a certain year, regional (governorate) and district (markaz) specifications are decided. Within each markaz, each local cooperative society is assigned certain production targets (area sown with specified crop) depending on size, location, etc. Within each local society, cropping-plans are then made for individual members which receive credit in kind and some cooperative services for producing those crops specified in the plan. When the local production plan is specified, it is exhibited in the society's office where members are given the opportunity to express their comments and eventually adjust the proposals. The local society's plan is then sent upwards through the cooperative hierarchy until it finally, after eventual further adjustments, is ratified by the Ministers of Supply and Agriculture. After the plan has been ratified, it is returned to the local cooperative where it is again exhibited and now has the status of binding law. To evade the plan and the crop rotation programme is punishable and it is the duty of the *mushrif* and the local board of directors to see to it that the plan is realized.

The reason why cooperative membership was made compulsory is sometimes said to be the reluctance of peasants' on 'old land' to voluntarily apply the 'scientific' system of consolidated block-farming and unified crop rotation. This is partly correct as the unified production system had some obvious disadvantages for the majority of smallholders. But the prime reason is not to be sought in the backwardness or 'traditionalism' of Egypt's peasantry. Rather, it is to be sought in Egypt's politico-economic development outside the agricultural sector.

COOPERATIVES AND THE REVOLUTIONARY GOVERNMENT AFTER 1952.

Much has been written about the 'Free Officers' lack of ideological commitment and political 'awareness' when *l'ancien régime* was overthrown in 1952 (see e.g. Chaliand 1977; Lacouture 1971; Olsen 1976; Wertheim 1972). Generally, the Revolutionary Command Council (RCC) has been described as a heterogeneous collection of young army officers "ranging from communists to extreme rightists" (Olsen 1976). Conventionally, it is therefore held that after an initial phase of liberal economic policy in the early 1950s, Egypt "drifted into

Arab Socialism between 1956 and 1961" (Hansen 1975). It is true that internal disputes and power struggles were intense before Nasser managed to consolidate his position as undisputed leader of the RCC. But rather than 'lack of awareness' it was the shortage of economic resources in combination with the circumstance that the *coup d'état* was a consequence of the actions of a small group, not of a mass movement, that determined the economic and political development of Egypt in the 1950s. We may thus agree with Robert Mabro that "despite a strong element of continuity in economic performance and the persistence of the old economic system, the first years of the Revolution in fact constitute a turning-point" when the foundations were laid for shaping a new "pattern of economic development, both in the short and long term" (Mabro 1974).

With no broad popular base, questionable legitimacy and no political programme except nationalism and a vague sense of the need for social reform, the new regime could not rely on mass-participation but set out to modernize the country from above. This, it must be underlined, was fully in line with prevailing development theory of that time, illustrated by statements like: "in countries like Egypt where the entrepreneurial class is a small one, the burden of undertaking important economic enterprises necessarily falls upon the state" (el-Brawy 1954). Initially, there were no attempts to change the economic system (except the limited Agrarian reform), which remained dominated by capitalism and private ownership throughout the 1950s (Mabro 1974). But while liberalism prevailed economically, politically it did not. Although the new regime was at first enthusiastically received by the masses, it had powerful opponents both inside and outside the country and it was too loosely founded to allow open political competition. The early Nasser government was convinced that "the people was not aware of its true interests" which "where known only to the revolutionaries and they could not permit the people to be mislead" (Rodinson 1968). For the new regime, then, 'modernization' was primarily a matter of managerialism and technology as is amply illustrated by the 'scientific' approach to agricultural development through state-supervised Agrarian Reform Cooperatives.

Several factors contributed to Nasser's radicalization around 1960. Initially, the new regime's capacity to undertake the necessary economic enterprise was limited. It was therefore hoped that, as the former class of large landowners was partially compensated for sequestrated land, and as the state largely refrained from interference in economic life outside agriculture, owners of capital would now turn to industrial investments. This did not occur and money was instead used for speculation in urban real estate, for imports of luxury goods for the wealthy few, or it was simply channeled out of the country.

Since 1955 Nasser had proved to be a master in playing one superpower against the other, thereby maximizing the financial flows from both, but from about

1960 it had become clear that this policy could no longer be pursued and that a choice had to be made between dependence on either the east or the west block. Although prior to the *coup* of 1952 Nasser had contacts with the CIA and the US government viewed the revolutionary command council as a shield against communism (Lacouture 1971), the choice was now the USSR. Among other things this led to a termination in western food-aid to the country.

Another reason for Nasser's radicalization at that time was that the US government revoked a loan (for the construction of a dam across the Nile for electrification and irrigation purposes) after the Egyptian arms-deal with Czechoslovakia in 1955. Nasser answered by nationalizing the Suez Canal and some foreign banks. Egypt lost the ensuing Suez-war of 1956 - but it won the Canal, the incomes of which were now to be used for the construction of the High Dam at Aswan, the symbol for independence, industrialization and modernization. Nasser's charisma was enormously boosted by this firm action against the aggression of foreign imperialists and in the years to follow Nasser's internal legitimacy came to depend heavily on such spectacular performance on the international political arena. Tempting as such foreign policy adventures were, they nevertheless lead to neglect of Egypt's internal development (Ajami 1982).

A contributing explanation of this radical, political reorientation is the Syrian break-away from the United Arab Republic in 1961 - largely a consequence of opposition from the Syrian bourgeoisie - which reminded Nasser of the strength of the bourgeoisie at home. Therefore he radicalized policy within Egypt itself. For both internal and external political reasons it thus became necessary to increase control over production as well as over people. Here, cooperatives seemed to provide a useful instrument.

Already in 1957, in a speech at a cooperative convention, Nasser had declared that the goal of the revolution was to create a *cooperative, democratic, socialist society* (Baker 1978; Treydte 1971). In the National Charter (1962), which outlined the new political programme for Egypt, Nasser defined the objectives of the Arab struggle as: "freedom, socialism, and unity", stating that "popular organizations, especially cooperatives and trade unions, were to play an important role in promoting democracy" (Nasser 1962). From then on, agricultural cooperatives became "the corner stone in the practical application of land reform" (Abu el-Kheir 1976). Today, leading representatives of the agricultural cooperative 'movement' call this period "the Golden Epoque" of cooperation in Egypt (Idris 1984) and foreign commentators have sometimes concluded that "Egypt's system of agrarian cooperatives is perhaps the only feature of Arab Socialism worth imitating" (Hansen 1975). The latter, however, seems highly questionable.

SOCIALISM AND COOPERATION IN THE 1960S.

Based on the somewhat exaggerated assumption of success with the Agrarian Reform cooperatives, the thrust of agricultural policy now became to spread this kind of cooperatives throughout the country (Baker 1978), and it has been stated that already within two years all Egypt's (at that time) 3,500 villages had been included in the scheme (Treydte 1971). It is generally claimed that 100% of the countryside is covered by cooperatives and that every village has an agricultural cooperative located within its domains. Such statements about a full spatial coverage of Egyptian agricultural cooperatives ought to be treated with caution, however.

Figure 2: Egypt's Central Place Hierarchy and Distribution of Agricultural Primary Cooperative Societies.

Greater Cairo
12-16 million inh.

20 intermed. cities
100,000-1 mill. inh.

85 small cities
20,000-100,000 inh.

5,000 "mother vill."
1,000-20,000 inh.

>30,000 "sattelite vill."
<1,000 inh.

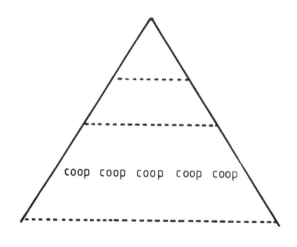

"Village" in Egypt is an administrative unit, sometimes with as many as 20,000 inhabitants. The village, or "mother village", is the lowest ranking level in the central place system recognized by the government, its administrative organs and planning units. Below the mother village level there are 30,000 to 40,000 "attached" or "satellite villages" administratively linked to their respective mother villages. It is in the 5,000 mother villages that the agricultural primary cooperatives are located. Thus, in a way it may be correct to claim that all Egyptian villages have a cooperative society within their domains. Noticing, however, that the number of attached villages is as high as over 30,000 and the vast number of people inhabiting such places, the rate of spatial cooperative coverage diminishes substantially. Less than 1/7 of Egypt's villages appear to have been provided with a cooperative society and as a rule primary societies serve several settlements. The reason for this is obviously that many attached villages are too small to constitute economically viable units. This need not be a severe practical problem as distances are mostly short and because attached villages already have other links to mother villages for various administrative purposes.

But problems arise as linkages between "satellite" and "mother" villages are not co-ordinated between different administrative or cooperative departments. Therefore, one satellite village may be attached to different mother villages for different administrative purposes, or it may belong to a "mother cooperative" in one village while at the same time it belongs to the local council of another mother village. Peasants thus, in their contacts with higher administrative levels, and usually lacking the means of transportation, are forced to spend unnecessary large amounts of time dealing with public authorities (including cooperatives) of various kinds. This confused situation is further aggravated by the prevailing pattern of land tenure and the thereupon based differentiation of cooperative categories. A peasant owning both "old land" and "Agrarian Reform land" thus belongs to two different agricultural cooperatives. The offices of these societies need not be located in the same mother village. But this is not all. Beside the different types of agricultural cooperatives, there also exist "Village Development Cooperatives" administered by the Ministry of Social Affairs, and Consumer Cooperatives related to the Ministry of Supply (sometimes, however, agricultural primary societies also run shops for consumer-goods). Also in this case, neither co-ordination nor joint location are necessary phenomena.

The strategy of extending the system of Agrarian Reform cooperatives to cover the whole country encountered sharp and revealing obstacles, rooted both in the mentioned overestimation of earlier success, and in underestimation of the problem of replacing the old system with these tightly controlled cooperatives in areas untouched by land reform. Implementing the system was fairly effective in Agrarian Reform and Land Reclamation areas where peasants had voluntarily joined the local cooperatives, and sometimes had moved to a new settlement in order to obtain land. But it was quite ineffective on 'old land' where social structures remained largely unchanged and landownership was more unequally distributed (Kirsch 1977). Those small-holders on 'old land' who were obliged to accept fixed rotation schemes after 1961 frequently found that their land had to be planted with only one crop in a given year. In case that crop was cotton they would not earn a profit and would have to wait one or two years to recoup losses. Readjustments thus became necessary and land exchanges were frequent. This again added to fragmentation of holdings but safeguarded the peasants' subsistence needs. In 1980, 98% of land-owners on 'old land' were found to possess land in more than one block (COPAC 1981). The frustration caused by such problems was further reenforced by the patriarchal attitudes of legislators and state authorities towards the peasants.

Around 1960 more than half Egypt's population was classified as rural. At present, Egypt's rural population amounts to more than 20 million people and now as then the vast majority of them are poor villagers. Virtually all villages are densely populated space-saving settlements with narrow unpaved streets and dwindling alleys, loosing themselves among mud-houses along canals which simultaneously are used for irrigation, washing, bathing, watering animals, and, as latrines and waste-dumps. As land is expensive (Egyptian farmland costs more than in Sweden or Great Britain), barns are rare, and animal feed, agricultural subsistence products and residuals (maize- and cotton-stalks) used as fire-wood are stored on roofs in layers sometimes several meters thick. Not only do these heaps of dry agricultural products attract rats, insects and occasional snakes, they are also highly inflammable, so a fire may easily wipe out a whole village. While, since the 1960s, the larger villages have usually become electrified and often have been provided with piped water, the smaller villages have hardly changed, still being "amongst the most insanitary and unhealthy places in the world to live" (Beaumont et al 1988). Village life is based on kinship solidarity and patriarchy. Also residence is kinship oriented with different sections, wards and quarters inhabited by the same agnatic group, a pattern which is reinforced by rather stringent rules on intermarriage. Village life is very much governed by an "economy of affection" of a kind very different from that described by Hydén in Africa south of the Sahara. "Religious and communal cleavages are basic to the structure of Middle East ... life and not simply anomalies or the result of imperfect assimilation" (Bates & Rassam 1983). Egyptian peasants have been "captured" (i.e. dominated and exploited) by more powerful classes and/or foreign colonizers since pharaonic days, which is why primordial groups, sufi-orders and the "affective economy" remain strong and serve as shields against suppression from above. Superimposed cooperatives and mandatory production regulations are not well fitted to serve these local socio-economic environments and peasants have found several ways to escape being trapped by the system.

An example of the difficulties associated with implementing the cooperatively administered triennial block-farming system in 'old land' villages is provided below. The Musha primary agricultural cooperative covers an area of 5,000 feddan of farmland in Upper Egypt. Land is divided into 4,500 individually owned parcels (too small to be shown on the map), but as tenancy is widespread, operated units only number 1,500 (Bösl 1984). As can be seen from map 2 land has not been divided into three blocks. Instead, it contains 64 larger fields separated by irrigation canals, and a number of consolidated blocks, each covering parts of several fields. Rather than indicating inefficiency in application of the theoretical model, this actually represents adaption to reality. If all Musha's land had been divided into three equally large blocks, each such block would have covered an area of 1,700 feddan. This would have meant

Map 2. Land-use in Musha Primary Cooperative Society.

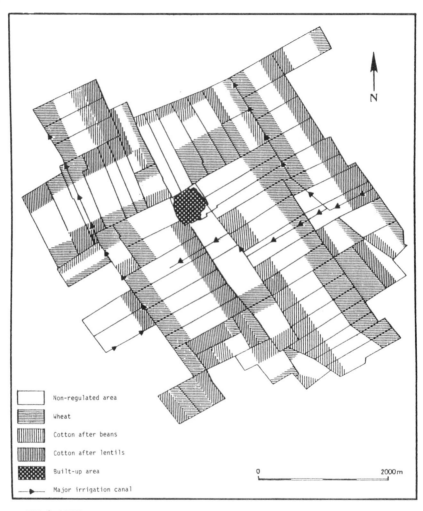

Non-regulated area

Wheat

Cotton after beans

Cotton after lentils

Built-up area

Major irrigation canal

N

0   2000 m

Source: Bösl, 1984.

large-scale mono-crop agriculture with greatly enhanced risks for plant diseases and infestation by parasites (in 1961 more than a third of the national cotton crop was destroyed by vocarious cotton leaf worms). The example from Musha shows that there has not been such great rigidity in applying the ideal crop rotation model as suggested in most presentations of Egyptian land-use patterns since the revolution.

On the other hand, map 2 also reveals that as much as 50% of the land belonging to this cooperative is excluded from the common crop rotation scheme. Large and very small landowners have found ways to evade the superimposed system. Peasants owning less than a feddan of farmland have been found not to be punished for evading the mandatory cropping regulations if they refer to subsistence needs in Islamic courts (Nasr 1983). 14% of the landowners in Musha own less than 1 feddan each (Hopkins 1983). They may therefore be excluded. Through bribery, clientelism or seats on the board of directors, large and medium-sized landowners have been able to avoid the system of enforced crop rotation, thereby being able to grow the more lucrative fruits and vegetables which are sold on the free market. In Musha 13 large landowners own more than 20 feddan each and 7 of them control units of more than 100 feddan each (Bösl 1984). These large holdings, or parts thereof, may also be excluded from the common crop rotation schemes. Thus, 25 years after the mandatory crop rotation system was introduced, it only applies to half the village land in this case. Furthermore, it only applies to land owned by small (above subsistence level) and lower-medium categories of landowners (>1-5 feddan). But even those who must plant according to the plan have frequently been found to prefer selling inputs like fertilizers and pesticides on the black market to those who can not obtain such products from the cooperatives. This increases peasant incomes but reduces yield-levels of required crops. Others have removed the topsoil on their fields, producing brick for construction purposes which, in the short run at least, is more profitable than farming. From a planning point of view, implementation of the system has not been efficient. But politically it has been very advantageous.

In spite of all 'socialist' rhetoric (and undeniable initial improvements for the poor) the main effect of Egypt's land reforms was to abolish the class of large absentee landowners, but the Nasser regime directly and indirectly also came to strengthen the rural middle-layers, owning 5 to 50 feddans, but constituting only 5% of the landowners. To a considerable degree the government came to depend on village elites and this group of 'medium-sized' landowners. These rural patrons quickly managed to dominate the cooperative boards of directors, diverting cooperative services to their own exclusive use. Nasser tried to curb such abuses by enacting a law that stated that 80% of the members of the boards of directors were to be held by peasants owning less than five feddans, i.e. those poor peasants believed to have a natural interest in socialism. As family, clan and patron-client relations are much more important in rural Egypt than class, this approach failed and the village elites, through patronage and other means, largely maintained their control over local cooperatives. Disappointed with the small peasants, the government's response was to appoint more public officials to run the cooperatives and to increase central control, thereby by-passing the locally elected boards of directors. This placed a heavy strain on public human and financial resources. First, the number of "supervised" cooperatives had increased from 104 to 3,500 in only two years, and now the numbers of appointed "inspectors" and other cooperative officials were again to increase manifold. There were not enough agronomists to satisfy these needs and many poorly educated were assigned to posts for which they had not been adequately prepared. Many such supervisors had, in fact, held the same positions on the former estates and/or belonged to the increasingly powerful rural middle class. As it turned out, also these officials were easily corrupted and dominated by local patrons.

This bureaucratization of the cooperative system reflects a general trend in national development, initiated during the Nasser era. When the Free Officers seized power in 1952, there was no social group outside the army that gave them immediate political support. Distribution (although limited) of land to small peasants served to overcome that. But even more so, a technocratic development strategy and the fast expansion of bureaucracy served to create "an artificial caste for which the regime's survival would be a necessity" (Baker 1978). Army officers were appointed to high administrative posts, but Nasser was also keen to favour "apolitical" engineers and technocrats for the management of development (Ayubi 1982; Garthon 1987). Some "liberal" politicians from the pre-1952 period were also co-opted into the new political machine[2] (Lacouture 1971; Springborg 1982). Top bureaucrats were sometimes appointed on the basis of merit, but in many cases primarily because they were loyal to Nasser. Even during Nasser's period of "Arab Socialism", it has been noted that "legitimized by neither socialist goals nor representative democratic procedures, the regime increasingly resorted to the carrots and stick-practices

---

2. That the revolution of 1952 did not end the political power of the old landed aristocracy - and that family, clientélism and personal networks remain more important in Egyptian politics than ideology or official institutions - is amply illustrated by the political career of Sayed Marei, formerly Minister of Agriculture, Speaker of the People's Assembly,"father of Agrarian Reform" and the architect behind Egypt's post-1952 agricultural cooperative system. Marei entered parliament as a provincial notable and large landowner under *l'ancien régime* in the 1940s. As a prominent politician, he survived both king Farouk and the two presidents Nasser and Sadat, and his career lasted well into the 1980s under the government of Hosny Mubarak. For a detailed review of Sayed Marei's political career, see Springborg 1982.

of favouritism and clientelism - in order to bolster the leadership's waning credibility and unstick the wheels of the vast state bureaucracy" (Moore 1986).

The absence of stable political institutions, the weak base of legitimacy for the government, and its reliance on this new "class" of public officials, and the top bureaucrats' perception of power as personal mandates, resulted in a system of *bureaucratic feudalism* with public office functioning as personal fiefdoms and lucrative satrapies within the expanding public administration. Bureaucracy was characterized by patronage and personal relations rather than by legal prescriptions, by rivalries between different blocks of power, by frequent changes of top bureaucrats and Ministers in order to limit their political autonomy, and by a severe lack of co-ordination between (and often within) Ministries and Departments (Ayubi 1982; Baker 1978; Springborg 1975, 1982). Cooperative organizations were no exceptions.

That politicians and top bureaucrats (at least for some time) displayed great ambitions to pursue their own highly diverging policies within their own respective domains - irrespective of stated national political objectives - may be exemplified with the al-Tahrir Province. Initiated in 1953, al-Tahrir (Liberation) Province constituted one of Egypt's major land reclamation areas and was also one of Nasser's grand monuments of progress and independence. The al-Tahrir Project Director, Magdi Hassanein, was a committed leftist hoping to transform class relations in rural Egypt, beginning from his base in the land-reclamation area under his command. Like Marei in the Agrarian Reform Authority, Hassanein had managed to circumvent normal bureaucratic and accounting regulations and was able to pay his followers several times the salaries paid in the ministries, thereby effectively boosting the support from his entourage. Reclaimed land was to be distributed to landless agricultural labourers, small peasants and demobilized soldiers in plots equal to those in Agrarian Reform areas (3-5 feddan per family). Hassanein, however, rather than promoting individual land ownership, saw the future for the poor rural classes in communal ownership and collectivized farming. Consequently he, semi-secretively, refused to distribute land and designed the Tahrir province as a "collective farm, further propagating communalism by forcing peasants to wear identical shirts and pants and having them sing ballads in praise of nationalism and socialism" (Springborg 1982).

While officially declaring that the agrarian reform model was soon to be implemented, he nevertheless refused to fulfil that promise, hoping to present a *fait accompli*. Many settlers finally reached a state of incipient rebellion but land was not distributed until after 1957 when Hassanein was fired and Sayed Marei, by many Egyptians known as a feudal reactionary, in his new capacity as Minister of Agriculture, went to pains to quickly terminate Egypt's only experiment in collective agriculture. From then on, the agricultural policy instead concentrated on spreading the system of supervised cooperatives over the country.

Within this bureaucratic structure, Egypt's system of agricultural cooperatives came to be modeled after the tightly controlled Agrarian Reform societies, but with separate organizations for the three different types of land cultivated: 'Old Land', Agrarian Reform land, and Reclaimed Land. Beside these three multi-purpose cooperative hierarchies, a further nine types of single-crop cooperative organizations were created to handle collection and marketing of specified, mandated, crops. Depending on types of land owned, and crops grown, the peasants belonged to one or more of these cooperative organizations. Responsibilities often overlapped and peasants found it difficult to grasp, not to mention deal with, this unwieldy cooperative super-structure. Bureaucratic awkwardness and conflicts between "technocrats" and "politicians" not only hampered efficiency, but drained resources that could have promoted development. This lack of resources was accentuated by restrictions caused by the "war economy" and the withdrawal of US development aid in 1964. The Egyptian economy faced a downward trend from the mid-1960s. Cooperatives increasingly came to be used as instruments for taxation of agriculture and paternalism probably increased. Through the system of mandatory cropping, state supervision, cooperative monopolies and fixed prices on inputs and output, the rate of implicit taxation of agriculture increased in the 1960s (Korayem 1981). Cooperative managers were "only concerned with the problem of obtaining as promptly as possible the settlement of the land taxes, annual instalments, and loans in kind or cash due by the members - rather than [with] the introduction of thorough and radical changes in the techniques and ways of life of the peasantry in their care" (Amin 1980).

The disastrous war of 1967 put a further strain on resources, it also weakened the government and, for some time, criticism was allowed to be aired. As the peasantry had become increasingly dissatisfied with routine procedures and services available to them through the rural institutions, calls for increased cooperative self-reliance mounted high. This resulted in the creation of a Central Agricultural Cooperative Union (CACU) in 1970 as an organization said to be the representative organ of all agricultural cooperatives. Rydberg states that, at that time, Egypt's small peasants, generally, displayed a "highly developed class-consciousness" (Rydberg 1975). To avoid the risk of the CACU being turned into an uncontrollable, radical, organization, president Nasser took steps to ensure that this upgrading of the cooperative system was only a cosmetic measure. Political leaders of the ASU were placed on the CACU board of directors, and CACU was "plagued by government interference from the onset" (Moharram 1983a).

COOPERATIVES AND OPEN ECONOMIC DOORS IN THE 1970S.

After the death of Nasser in 1970, Anwar Sadat, managed to consolidate his position as president and more or less autocratic ruler of Egypt. Like Nasser before him, Sadat tended to depend heavily on 'chock diplomacy' and spectacular performances on the international political arena for the legitimization of internal power. Even more than Nasser, he came to rely on availability of external economic resources and, in this pursuit, reoriented Egypt's foreign policy 180 degrees. Substituting dependence on the USA with that on the USSR, and "opening the doors" of Egypt for transnational corporations and (expected) investments from the conservative oil-rich Arab Gulf States, Sadat was (in spite of much rhetoric to the contrary) reluctant to liberate Egypt internally - at least not immediately and especially not politically. Being a less self-evident national leader than Nasser, Sadat found it necessary to counterbalance the upper echelons of bureaucracy by rehabilitating "many agents and politicians from *l'ancien régime*, corrupt businessmen and big landlords who had attempted to resist the Agrarian Reform" (Amin 1978). Quite surprisingly, this was done at the same time as Sayed Marei, the "father of Agrarian Reform", turned out to be one of Sadat's most important and powerful political allies.

As part of Sadat's "corrective revolution" a reorganization of the cooperatives was announced. In May 1971 cooperative elections, heavily imprinted by government pressures, were held and an extensive programme for upgrading the cooperative system was launched under the new CACU-chairman Ahmad Yunis. Although it seems as if Yunis took this responsibility seriously, this again turned out to be meant merely as a cosmetic measure and the programme came to a halt already after a few years. While in the declaration of his political programme, the "October Working Paper" (1974), Sadat placed much future hope on the private sector and severely criticized the performance of the public sector, he only had the following to say about the cooperative sector: "The cooperative sector in agriculture and crafts is also in need of a strong drive so as to keep pace with the sought rates of development" (Sadat 1974). Sadat neither expected much from, nor paid much attention to, agricultural cooperatives.

The irony of Sadat's *Infitah* (the "open door" policy) is that to allow the intended economic reorientation - bureaucratic deregulation and partial dismantling of the public sector - he first found it necessary to increase control over both economic and political life. Thus, the "October Working Paper" on the one hand states that "an open door economy enhances the importance of planning", and on the other hand stresses the need for "national unity and national harmony", evident in Sadat's rejection of "the call for breaking up national unity in an artificial way through creating parties" (ibid). As far as agriculture was concerned, this meant more technocratic managerialism and reduced cooperative self-reliance in combination with favourable treatment of the village elites and medium size landowners together with a rehabilitation of the former upper class. The Agrarian Reform itself came under attack. In June 1975 an amendment to the Agrarian Reform Law "put rents up 25%, authorized owners to evict tenants who fell into arrears, and entrusted to tribunals the arbitration of disputes which until then had fallen under the jurisdiction of rural committees which had been more closely linked with the peasants" (Amin 1978; see also Waterbury 1978).

1976 saw the dissolvement of the CACU by presidential decree after frequently reported accusations of economic malpractices at high cooperative levels. Sums of money as large as £E 60 million were said to have "disappeared". With these accusations of economic dishonesty in the cooperative leadership "more as pretext than cause" (Waterbury 1978), the CACU was immediately liquidated, its directors fired and the chairman put in confinement. The cooperatives were administratively placed directly under the Ministry of Agriculture and supply of agricultural credit was transferred to the government owned Principal Bank for Development and Agricultural Credit (PB-DAC). As a result, not many activities remained for the cooperatives which, as they lost commissions on sales of inputs and marketing of products, faced a trend of diminishing returns (Ismail & Toll 1978).

Various explanations of the cooperative crisis in 1976 have been presented and usually embezzlement is taken for granted (see e.g. Kirsch 1977; Kirsch et al 1980). However, behind the official reasons heavy political power struggles can be discerned. A former Under-secretary for Cooperatives explained that "Yunis and the CACU violated the cooperative principle of neutrality (*sic!*) and tried to interfere in politics. Therefore, they needed a reprimand" (personal interview). The announced upgrading of the cooperative system and the alleged rapprochement to the cooperative principles was never intended to turn the cooperatives into an independent member organization. On the contrary, the measure's prime objective was to calm the peasantry, to disarm opposition and to re-establish governmental control over the country's largest economic sector. When the CACU leadership began to act as a political pressure group, the period of cooperative liberalization rapidly came to an end.

Meanwhile, the juridical investigations of the embezzlement case continued and the court did not reach a final decision until after six years. By then, both Yunis and Sadat were dead. The accused were freed on all charges and in 1982 the court declared that "the whole struggle was politically motivated due to the Union's attempts to secure more freedom for the cooperatives and to free them from governmental dominance" (Moharram 1983a). A new CACU board of directors was elected, but it had been clearly demonstrated to everyone where independent cooperative activity would lead to. The new CACU chairman is not the political fighter that Yunis was and, to be sure, when elected, he was deprived of those possibilities to establish an independent political platform that Yunis had enjoyed. He was Yunis successor in the Peoples' Assembly but upon becoming chairman of the CACU his nomination was not renewed. He also lost his position as Secretary General of the ASU. Thus, the new CACU had its wings clipped before being re-established in 1983.

While the Union was dissolved in 1976, these events did not imply the liquidation of cooperative societies at local and regional levels. These societies remained but functioned more as parastatals than as cooperatives. Rather than constituting a frontal attack on bureaucratic mismanagement, the cooperative crisis in the 1970s represented "a refined phase of centralization" (Hopkins 1983) and for six years there was no representative cooperative organ that could formulate cooperative policy or safeguard peasant interests. Supply of credit was transferred to the PBDAC, but for the peasants the bank was found to be "as corrupt as the cooperatives" (Nadim 1979).

Meanwhile, the Egyptian economy deteriorated further. In 1982 an ILO-study revealed that "in terms of industrialization, the economy is hardly more advanced than it was 20 years ago [and that] the share of industry has, if anything, even declined during the past five years" (Hansen & Radwan 1982). The ineffective public sector not only remained overwhelmingly dominant, but its share of total employment continued to grow while bureaucratic performance deteriorated even further, partly as a consequence of "a mass of legal controls which are providing an obstacle to its efficient running" (Wahba 1983). Other obstacles to bureaucratic efficiency were overstaffing, very low salaries, excessively slow action, apathy, and lack of discipline (Ayubi 1982; Leila et al 1985).

While investments in agriculture were kept at a very low level and industrialization stagnated or even declined, and while the "open door" economic policy did not attract the expected amounts of foreign investment (Ikram 1980), Sadat was forced to continue Nasser's "social welfare guarantees" in the form of subsidized basic consumer goods (particularly bread) and guarantees of public employment for the educated. While this was a necessary price to pay to avoid social unrest (as exemplified by the food riots in 1977), this policy came to place an ever increasing strain on public finance, and came increasingly to be financed from external "development aid". Bruton has described the Egyptian economy at the end of the Sadat era as being in a "state of limbo" where physical planning was even less effective than earlier, and with "no satisfactory market mechanism having evolved to take its place" (Bruton 1983). A fairer assessment of the "open door" economic policy in general would be to say that Sadat's new economic policy amounted to "no less than minimum government involvement in socio-economic development" [except, as we have seen, a tighter control over the cooperatives and the small-holders] (Ibrahim 1982).

Instead of actively trying to "take charge" of development and direct it in a certain direction, Sadat sought external solutions to internal problems while at the same time he was buying political support from the upper classes with these external financial resources. Sadat's westward turn, especially after the Camp David agreement, invited large-scale US involvement in Egyptian development and policy formulation, and dramatically increased US development "aid". The US is presently deeply engaged in the modernization of Egyptian agriculture and rural institutions. Discussions with USAID-staff in Cairo reveal, however, that the US does not want anything to do with cooperatives which are seen as stepping stones towards communism. A report submitted to the US Congress in 1978 declared that "perhaps best left to its own decline, cooperative structure ... should be gradually replaced by modern, private business mechanisms, and, locally, by Village Banks [i.e. PBDAC offices] and similar credit funds" (quoted in Waterbury 1978). This, as we have seen, is exactly what happened. In spite of all "liberal" and "anti-authoritarian" rhetoric, US involvement in Egyptian affairs under the Sadat regime did not speed up democratization or provide better opportunities for the poor. On the contrary, "the United States, as one of the great powers of the globe, has done nothing to deter this trend towards authoritarianism and capitalism, if it has not actually encouraged it" (Waterbury 1983).

The rate of agricultural taxation actually declined in the 1970s, but this was largely a consequence of increased subsidization of imported fertilizers, not of raised producer prices which were still kept extremely low (Korayem K 1981). Governmental price and credit policies were increasingly geared in favour of the minority of larger landowners. Subsidized fodder concentrates are, due to government regulations, only sold to farmers owning five cattle or more - 95% of the Egyptian peasants own less than five heads of cattle! Likewise, while the small peasants would, through the PBDAC, only receive credit in kind for unprofitable, mandated crops, subsidized credit for productive investments is given only to the same group of wealthy landowners. The PBDAC provides loans for the purchase of tractors only to owners of at least five feddan of farmland - 95% of the Egyptian landowners own less than five feddan!

An important task for the "scientifically supervised" agricultural cooperatives has been to introduce modern farming techniques to the peasantry. However, extension services have been found presently to be "virtually non-existent" (Commander 1987). A case study of cooperative education in the delta revealed that 81% of those interviewed had not received any information at all about new agricultural methods (el-Haydary 1983). Neglect of agricultural extension is almost total. Not only has cooperative education almost completely been directed towards the training of "leaders" and officials, with an outspoken emphasis on legislation and neglect of the meaning of cooperation. Not only is it a general observation in Egypt that "a majority ... of university graduates employed by the government are required to work in departments other than those for which they have been trained" (Yassin 1983). Furthermore, while the Ministry of Agriculture employs around 150,000 people, but the National Extension Service (MOA-branch) only provides 2,000-2,200 extension agents to Egypt's 3.5 million peasants in 5,000 local agricultural cooperative societies (IADS 1984). In gross figures, thus, each extension officer has to serve 2.5 cooperative societies and more than 1,500 peasants. In practice, however, the situation is even worse as there is "a concentration of agents in Cairo, most of whom are without field experience" (Ikram 1980).

While the cooperatives were to provide mechanical services and equipment to the peasants, this aspect of modernization has been almost totally neglected. In 1979 cooperatives only owned 10% of the tractors in Egypt, and many of these were in a state of deterioration. Thus, instead of hiring out tractor services to their members and keeping the prices for mechanized services down, the small peasants, and even cooperative societies, have been forced to rent tractor services from the wealthy landowners at high prices. At the same time, it has been much easier for the larger landowners to circumvent the central cropping regulations than for the smallholders . Corruption and black market transactions have flourished in spite of (and sometimes with the support of) the huge control apparatus. At the end of the 1970s it was concluded that "the small scale farming unit can be highly profitable; it depends largely to what extent the farmer can sell his produce on the black market" (Holdsworth 1980). What was fostered during the 1970s, if anything, must be deemed as the opposite of a cooperative "ethos". Concerning the governments of both Nasser and Sadat, which witnessed three revolutions (a political revolution in 1952, a "socialist" revolution in 1961, and a "corrective" revolution in 1971), we can agree with Baker that "for Egypt's peasants there has been no revolution" (Baker 1978).

POLITICAL LIBERALIZATION AND COOPERATIVES IN THE 1980S.

Under the rule of president Mubarak, the realization that something has to be done to reverse this trend has become widespread and important steps have been taken to improve rural and cooperative conditions. Where these steps will lead to is less clear, however.

Presently, Egypt is passing through a phase of "*perestrojka*" - the "open door" economic policies are being continued and political freedom is being introduced. The aim is an eventual dismantling of the public sector, encouragement of private enterprise, and the establishment of political pluralism. Such an overall politico-economic climate may permit cooperatives to function as genuine, member-oriented, self-help institutions. The fact that cooperative membership is no longer compulsory is definitely a step in that direction. Central pricing policy has been improved and, in the last few years, producer prices have been raised for most crops. Forced deliveries have been abolished except for cotton and half the rice harvest. In March 1987 the Minister of Agriculture explained that the goal also is to "remove government crop area controls". The exchange rate of the over-valued Egyptian Pound has been set at the previously dominating black market rate, a measure which not only guarantees that the State receives some of the remittances, through bank deposits, from Egypt's more than three million labour migrants, but which also favours export and productive investment rather than import and speculation.

Parliamentary elections, allowing competition from opposition parties, have been held in 1984 and 1987. Although regulations favoured the president's party, these elections have by many been deemed unusually fair by Middle East standards. Thus, it has been concluded that Egypt now "has passed the early populist stage" (Hinnebuch 1981). The above mentioned measures have caused Garthon for example to declare that Mubarak's Egypt "not only is a democracy. It is a former revolutionary one-party state that by peaceful and legal means has transformed itself into a democracy" (Garthon 1987). Within these parameters, some writers on cooperation in Egypt do not hesitate to declare that the agricultural cooperatives are now being turned into self-help organizations (Abd el-Rahman 1983; Nau 1983). What then has actually happened "inside" the cooperatives during the present decade?

A new Law on Agricultural Cooperatives (No 122/1980) was enacted in 1980 and the CACU was re-established in 1983 as representative organ of all agricultural cooperative organizations. The new law defines cooperation as a "popular democratic movement promoted by the state, and which contributes to the implementation of the state's overall policy". Cooperative societies are defined as "socio-economic units who ... operate ... within the framework of the State's overall plan" (1). The same law also states that cooperative societies are "any society constituted ... by their own choice and as is consistent with the cooperative principles internationally acknowledged..." (2).

There is a contradiction between these two paragraphs and it is not clear whether cooperatives are to be regarded as governmental or member organizations. The present government's attitude towards cooperatives remains rather ambivalent (Holmén 1985), reflecting the "general confusion regarding the aims to be followed by the public sector in Egypt, and regarding the intentions of the government and policy makers towards the sector" (Wahba 1983). Membership in cooperatives is presently a voluntary matter and peasants can choose whether they want to use cooperatives or the "Village Bank" to obtain credit. In case they use the cooperative, this only functions as an intermediary between the bank and the peasant, and credit terms are still determined by the State. The cooperative "movement" is permitted to establish its own bank, but this has not yet occurred.

Although this cooperative legislation was enacted in 1980 and the CACU re-established in 1983, the 5-Year Development Plan for 1982-87 did not mention cooperatives or their role in development. Neither did the Minister of Agriculture mention the role of cooperatives in his outlining of Egypt's agricultural development strategy for the 1980s (Wally et al 1982). The first time in the history of Egyptian national development planning that agricultural cooperatives were ever mentioned was in the sub-plan for 1983/84 and then only as "a complementary to the public and private sectors" (Moharram 1984)! The present national 5-Year development Plan, 1987-92, is much clearer and states that "rural institutions, agricultural cooperatives in particular, must be developed and strengthened to play an effective role in rural development" (GOE 1987).

Whether Egypt's agricultural cooperatives will actually be decontrolled and permitted to function as self-help institutions remains to be seen. Even if they are, the risk still remains that the cooperative organizations will again be turned into clubs for village and bureaucratic notables. Informal dependencies and patron-client relations are still the basic organizational institutions both in bureaucracy (Springborg 1982) and in rural Egypt (Hopkins 1987).

After this rather unpromising resumé of Egyptian development and the history of Egypt's agricultural cooperatives, it may seem quite astonishing that peasants' attitudes towards agricultural cooperatives have in several studies proved to be quite positive (el-Haydary 1983; Moharram 1983b; Nasr 1983). There are some restrictions to this, however, as members' goal perception primarily emphasizes the material aspects of cooperation, not the participatory aspects (el-Haydary 1983). Members attend meetings, but seldom participate in discussion (Moharram 1983b), a circumstance that, against the presented background, is quite understandable. Nevertheless, "the strong willingness of cooperative members to utilize educational cooperative services suggests an accessible origin for change, and thus a means by which to improve the cooperative system"(Blond 1984).

Another such accessible origin for change and a possible foundation for a new cooperative movement can be found in the small satellite village Basaisa in the heart of the Nile delta. Until recently, the entire economy of this hamlet was based on agriculture and the inhabitants were poor smallholders. Since 1980, the villagers have found a niche, uncontrolled by government authorities, where they have been able to experiment in voluntary association for economic enterprise and village services. An independent local village development cooperative has been established. While carefully avoiding direct agricultural activities so as not to catch the "evil eye" of the State, the cooperative has, through a system of collective savings and credit, been able to raise funds for investments in activities complementary to the controlled agricultural sector. This has added new enterprises to the village, broadened its economic base, created new job opportunities for the previously unemployed, and increased the standard of living for the villagers. Active participation in the cooperative now includes all households and has had great integrating impact, resulting in community gradually being substituted for family or clan as the major focus for solidarity. The experienced social soundness and economic viability of this self-help oriented cooperative society has attracted the attention of people in nearby villages. At present more than half the members come from villages other than Basaisa. Likewise, Basaisa has attracted many visitors from other (sometimes distant) villages who want to transplant the idea to their own places of residence.

The Basaisa local development cooperative is not only an economic organization. Basaisa is an "attached village", too small to have its own local council or its own agricultural cooperative society. Administratively it therefore belongs to a nearby "mother village" and for normal agricultural purposes to a cooperative in another nearby village, both situated 3-4 kms away. In order to facilitate contacts with various public officials, located in a variety of places (and often not even there during office time), the Basaisa cooperative board of directors also functions as an intermediary between villagers and bureaucracy, i.e. as a local council. When asked if this measure, or the economic projects in the village, attracted bureaucratic interference, a board member told me that "there is no problem since officials don't do their job". That was also one of the reasons why the cooperative was established in the first place. The astonishing solution to the problems of distance friction, officials' absenteeism and bureaucratic inefficiency in general is that the inhabitants of Basaisa have voluntarily created one extra administrative level as a means of rationalization! Obviously, such innovations could not be administered from above and it is doubtful whether it is replicable in other localities. But for once local authorities are responsible to their constituencies and the villagers do not have to spend as much time and effort on individual transportations to different public and cooperative authorities as they previously used to. These experiences indicate that the propensity among Egyptian smallholders to engage in formalized cooperative activities is great - provided the activities evolve as responses to felt needs and that they are permitted to run their own affairs.

Another important factor contributing to the eventual emergence of a "true" cooperative movement in Egypt is that, as a result of the cooperative crisis in 1976-82 when the cooperatives were deprived of most of their incomes, village notables have turned elsewhere when seeking to dominate public officials and divert public resources to their own exclusive use. Presently, "officials attached to the agricultural cooperatives lack both the supplies and the expertise to attract the 'attention' of local parties. They are thus more superfluous than dominant in terms of the local power structure" (Adams 1986). This situation may change rapidly if cooperatives were again to cater mainly to governmental 'needs' and to rely on public finances. But if cooperatives do develop into genuine self-help institutions, relying on their own resources, that risk will probably be much smaller, and the rural elite will most likely find more lucrative objects to exploit in a liberated economy.

With the re-establishment of the CACU in 1983, however, measures were taken to impede the transformation of cooperatives into independent institutions. The potential powerbase of the new, elected, CACU chairman was substantially reduced in 1983. Parallel to the cooperative member organization (the Union branch) there is still found a corresponding hierarchy of controlling cooperative departments within the Ministry of Agriculture (the Government branch). This Cooperative Department still employs the local cooperative managers and has the duty to supervise and inspect cooperatives at all levels. But government control also occurs "behind the curtain". In 1984 the Director General of the Cooperative Department within the Ministry of Agriculture also held the position as General Manager of the CACU. As he explained it, he was "on temporary loan from the Ministry on a part-time basis" (personal interview). The same was the case also with the staff employed in the CACU central office (Karlén et al 1984). Other governmental measures making it more difficult for the CACU to pursue independent goals are for example juridical prescriptions that all agricultural cooperative branches at national and regional levels shall be represented on the CACU board of directors. In 1984 this resulted in a CACU board of directors consisting of 105 persons. For the running of daily affairs this is a virtually unmanageable crowd and it definitely does not increase CACU efficiency. Instead, it greatly (unofficially) enhances the power of the General Manager and a small clique of Cairo-based tycoons - especially as travel expenses are not paid to board members from the countryside.

Other recent measures to 'strengthen' the Egyptian cooperative 'movement' include the enacting of a law (No 28/1984) leading to the creation of a General Cooperative Union (GCU) in 1984. This Union is intended to function as an apex organization and policy instrument for all cooperative sectors in Egypt, being made up of the National Cooperative Unions for Agriculture, Fishing, Housing, Crafts and Services. Whether this is really what Egypt needs ought to be a matter of debate.

WHITHER COOPERATIVES?

While cautious but positive expectations concerning the liberalization of cooperative may sometimes be discerned among Egypt's 3.5 million 'ordinary' cooperative members in the 5,000 cooperative societies, the present policy redirection has aroused a sense of euphoria among leading cooperative elements (Holmén 1987). A "golden" cooperative future is outlined in recent cooperative publications. First of all, the need to establish a cooperative bank (either agricultural or for the whole cooperative sector) is commonly stressed as this would provide the foundation for an independent movement (Moharram 1984; Rashad 1983). A common and integrated development strategy is also advocated for all cooperative organizations and the GCU is enthusiastically welcomed (Abu el-Kheir 1984). It is stressed that this consolidated cooperative sector must be guided by "scientific management" and use "scientific methods". Thus, it is again to be managed by technocrats.

At the same time a certain caution is evident as all these proponents underline that cooperatives are to operate within the bounds of the State's overall plan. Rashad goes even further and declares that "cooperatives should urge their members ... to deliver the fixed quota as a national duty" (Rashad 1983). Apart from that, there is generally a great caution about spelling out what a new and consolidated cooperative development strategy would include. It is symptomatic that a recent publication from the CACU about "the role of farmers' cooperatives" actually does not reveal anything about the role of cooperatives (CACU 1986). Among the future cooperative activities envisaged by leading cooperators in contemporary Egypt are instead mentioned, for example, "cheap pilgrimage travels, touristic and cultural tours and cooperative camping at sea-shores" (Rashad 1983). With the possible exception of the first of these, such enterprises can hardly be of major interest for the ordinary Egyptian peasant. Such "expectations" actually tell us very little about what is to become of a liberated cooperative movement in the future. But they do indicate some risks.

While paying lip-service to participation, these current cooperative writings reveal a very wide gap between the ordinary peasant members and their urban representatives. Integration of the various national cooperative unions under the aegis of a brand new super-union is bound to provide many well paid jobs for the educated few. While such opportunities for personal advancement are currently being created, further adding to the already top-heavy structure of Egyptian bureaucracy, it remains questionable whether recent development will also lead to extended member participation and influence in local cooperative matters. Life and world-views in villages and among the peasantry are very different from those found in Cairo's air-conditioned offices and limousines. A cooperative leadership dressed in gold-plated spectacles and expensive suits (western fashion) now sees a possibility to promote the "movement" and shape the future cooperative policy in negotiations with government officials and representatives of the emerging private sector companies. It seems as if, within a liberated cooperative "movement", state appropriation of agricultural surplus will be replaced by a semi-private urban elite siphoning off the wealth created by the agricultural sector, cooperatives again being turned into instruments for already wealthy strata.

We have found signs of positive attitudes towards cooperation among the Egyptian peasantry as well as a fruitful experiment with cooperative self-help in niches of the economy not controlled by government, and we have found attempts to liberate cooperative organizations at the macro level. But instead of placing too much hope on the central cooperative leadership and their abilities - or willingness - to promote a "true" cooperative "ethos" at the village level, we may note Hopkins words that the ordinary "Egyptian village credit cooperative [does not] represent the outcome of a social movement; nor is there today a social movement that supports them (Hopkins 1983). We have also seen tendencies within the cooperative elite at the national level to use signs of liberalization for creating new well-paid "co-ordinating" jobs for themselves within the cooperative superstructure, rather than taking the opportunity to build a new cooperative movement from below. But, whatever the risk of cooperatives being exploited by powerful "representatives", the major threats presently facing the Egyptian peasantry and the newly found cooperative liberty do not so much emanate from a distant, urban and well-paid cooperative "elite" or its possibly "liberal" interpretations of the meaning of cooperation. Rather, it is to be found in the overall precarious socio-economic situation prevailing in the country.

Egypt's physical and demographic situation has become accentuated during the late 20th century. With 96% of the area being made up of desert, arable land amounts to only 2.5 million ha, giving Egypt one of the highest man/land ratios in the world. Although expensive programmes have been launched to expand the cultivable area, it has been impossible to keep pace with population growth which presently adds about 100 000 new inhabitants each month. Thus, while in the 20th century arable land has increased by 20%, population has increased by 400%, and urban population by 900%. Total population has presently passed the 50 million level and is expected to reach 75 million at the turn of the century (SBW 1986). In that year the urban population will equal today's total population. On the one hand this means a dramatic increase in non-agricultural population which somehow has to be fed. On the other hand it means a rapid urban sprawl with severe threats to agricultural lands.

Urban sprawl already reduces agricultural land by about 0,5% annually (Commander 1987). Moreover, water-logging and salination further reduces the quality of the available soil (Kishk 1986). The area reclaimed for agricultural purposes at high costs since the 1950s (900,000 feddan) has been almost totally offset by such losses (700,000 feddan) during the same period. Agricultural investments have been kept at a low level and for some major crops, levels of production have stagnated during the 1980s (GOE 1987). National self-sufficiency has declined steadily since the introduction of the "open door" economic policy (SAAD-report 1982). Egypt today, therefore, imports half its food requirements (MEED July 1983) and 75% of its wheat needs (MEED March 1983). It is difficult to see how this trend could be reversed even if agricultural investments were substantially raised.

During the last years important steps have been taken to liberalize Egypt politically and economically. The present regime maintains the *Infitah*-policy at the same times as it promotes political pluralism. In this context, cooperative membership has not only become a voluntary matter, the government has also declared its intention to strengthen agricultural cooperative societies. Both within and outside Egypt this has aroused expectations of a new golden cooperative epoque. Economic and political liberalization have led several writers to declare that Egypt of today qualitatively differs from the Egypt of 10 or 20 years ago. It is thus held that the government presently rests on "true" legitimacy and that the regime now has passed its early populist and authoritarian stage.

However, while a certain degree of political liberty is undeniable, harsh treatment and even police-torture of certain political opposition groups are still frequently reported. Furthermore, while political opposition parties are allowed, legislation regulating political life still contains important populist stipulations. Thus, all parties must be "national" parties. Regional, sectoral, class-based or other "unnatural" creations are not permitted to openly compete for political power. Not only do such stipulations dramatically reduce influence and democratic participation. The prime purpose is, as was the case under Nasser and Sadat, to create an artificial sense of unity and national harmony. Likewise, while economic liberalization no doubt expands the scope for private and cooperative enterprise in the country, it has been noted that the *Infitah*-policy "pushes ... not so much toward private ownership as toward an oligarchic, protected, but nonetheless market-driven economy" (Moore 1986). Privatization, in its initial stages at least, should therefore be viewed "primarily as a political tactic for sustaining authoritarian regimes rather than as a set of reforms for stimulating free enterprise or markets" (ibid). In spite of the steps already taken to liberalize the country politically and economically, Egypt still has a long way to go before an environment is created where cooperative self-help organizations can thrive.

Growing socio-economic cleavages and increasingly unequal opportunities have caused social discontent to spread rapidly. Land hunger has forced poor peasants to occupy government-owned land-reclamation areas as squatters (The Egyptian Gazette, March 30, 1987). Demonstrations and riots have occurred on several occasions throughout the 1970s and 1980s when subsidies on basic consumer goods (notably bread) have been threatened. Violent protests against the conspicuous life-style of the westernized noveaux riches -the *Infitah-class* - resulted in the burning of several luxury hotels in Cairo in 1986. Dependence on the US has led to anti-american feelings being expressed in both the parliament, the press and the streets, and has even led to armed attacks on US diplomatic personnel. Social discontent nurtures religious fundamentalism which is spreading rapidly. However, it does not only direct itself against foreign influence and the westernized elite. Clashes between Copts and Muslims (with several deaths reported) have repeatedly taken place during the last few years.

Whether, in this precarious situation, there will really be room for further politico-economic liberalization, for the spreading of economic opportunities to the masses, not to mention for a strengthened and independent cooperative movement to pursue development goals from below without government interference and control, does indeed seem questionable. It is not at all improbable that the political threats, caused by the prevailing socio-economic frustration, will again be used as pretext for increased governmental effort to control popular organizations - among them cooperatives.

LITERATURE

Abd el-Rahman, A. (1983) *Agricultural Co-operation in Egypt*. Omar Lotfy Training Centre, Ismailiya.

Abdussallam, A.A., Abusedra, F.S. (1985) 'The Colonial Economy: Libya, Egypt and the Sudan'. In *General History of Africa VII - Africa Under Colonial Domination 1880-1935*. Ed. A Adu Boahen, UNESCO, Heinemann, London.

Abu el-Kheir, K.H. (1976) *Statement on Co-operative Structure in the ARE*. Cairo.

Abu el-Kheir, K.H. (1984) *A New Strategy for Developing the Co-operative System in Egypt*. Cairo, in Arabic.

Adams, R.J. (1986) Bureaucrats, Peasants and the Dominant Coalition: An Egyptian Case Study. In *The Journal of Development Studies, Vol. 22, No. 2*, pp 336-355.

Ajami, F. (1982) *The Arab Predicament - Arab Political Thought and Practice Since 1967*. Cambridge University Press, New York.

Amin, G. (1980) *The Modernization of Poverty - a study in the political economy of growth in nine Arab countries*. E.J. Brill, Leiden.

Amin, S. (1978) *The Arab Nation - Nationalism and Class Struggles*. Zed Press, London.

Ayubi, N. (1982) 'Bureaucratic Inflation and Administrative Inefficiency: the Deadlock in Egyptian Administration'. In *Middle Eastern Studies, Vol. 18, No. 3.* pp 286-299. London.

Baker, R.W. (1978) *Egypt's Uncertain Revolution under Nasser and Sadat.* Harvard University Press, Cambr. Mass./London.

Baker, R.W. (1981) 'Sadat's Open Door. Opposition from Within'. In *Social Problems, Vol. 28, No. 4,* pp. 378-384.

Blond, R.D. (1983) (ed.) *The Accomplishments of a California-Egypt Research Collaboration: The Agricultural Development Systems - Egypt Project 1979-1983.* USAID/MOA-Egypt/AC Davis.

Bonow, M. (1969) *Demokratisk Ekonomi.* Rabén & Sjögren, Uddevalla.

Von Braun, J., de Haen, H. (1983) *The Effects of Food Price and Subsidy on Egyptian Agriculture.* Res. Rep. 42. Intnl Food Policy Inst. Washington DC.

Bruton, H.J. (1983) 'Egypt's Development in the Seventies'. In *Economic Development and Social Change, Vol. 31, No. 4,* pp 679-703.

Bösl, K. (1984) 'Müsha - Struktur und Entwicklung eines ägyptischen Dorfes'. *Geographishe Rundschau, 36 (1984) H5,* pp. 248-254.

Castle, M.A. (1976) *Social Reproduction and the Egyptian Agrarian Transformation.* New York University.

CACU (1986) *Agricultural Pricing Policies and: the Role of Farmers' Co-operatives.* Central Agricultural Co-operative Union of Egypt. Cairo.

Chaliand, G. (1977) *Revolution in the Third World: Myths and Prospects.* The Harvester Press, Hassocks.

Commander, S. (1987) *The State and Agricultural Development in Egypt since 1973.* Ithaca Press, London.

COPAC (1981) *Co-operative Information Note: Arab Republic of Egypt.* COPAC, Rome.

DI (1987) *Dagens Industri.* March 4.

Dülfer, E. (1975) (ed.) *Zur Krise der Genossenschaften in der Entwicklungspolitik.* pp 1-16. Marburger Schriften zum Genossenschaftswesen. Reihe B/Band 10. VandenHoeck & Ruprecht, Göttingen.

Elbrawy, R. (1954) 'Some Problems of Economic Planning in the Middle East with Special reference to Egypt'. In *Middle East Economic Papers*, 1954. pp 26-36. American University in Beirut.

el-Haydary, A. (1983) *Der Einfluss der Ländlichen Genossenschaftstypen in Ägypten auf die Bildung und ausbildung ihrer Mitglieder.* Justus-Liebig-Universität, Giessen.

Fisher, W.B. (1987) 'Egypt'. In *The Middle East and North Africa 1988.* Europa Publ. Ltd. London.

Garthon, P. (1976) 'Egypten av idag'. In *Egypten.* Ed. T. Säve-Söderberg, Verbum, Stockholm.

Garthon, P. (1987) *Egypten - en arabisk demokrati.* Ordfront, Stockholm.

GOE (1981) *Agricultural Co-operative Law, No 122/1980.* Government of Egypt, Cairo.

GOE 1984) *Law on General Co-operative Union, No 28/1984.* Government of Egypt, Cairo.

GOE (1987) *5-year Development Plan 1987-92.* Government of Egypt, Cairo.

Hanel, A. (1985) 'Instruments of Self-Help Promotion - an Introduction into the Subject Matter'. In *Promotion of Self-Help Organizations.* pp. 179-199. Konrad Adenauer Stiftung. St Augustin.

Hansen, B. (1975) 'Arab Socialism in Egypt'. In *World Development. Vol. 3, No. 4*, pp 201-211.

Hansen, B. and Radwan, S. (1982) *Employment Opportunities and Equity in Egypt.* ILO, Geneva.

Hinnebuch, R.A. (1981) 'Egypt under Sadat: Elites, Power Structure, and Political Change in a Post-Populist State'. In *Social Problems. Vol. 28, No. 4*, pp 442-464.

125

Hirschfeld, A. (1980) 'Self-Development and Co-operation'. In *Co-operation as an Instrument for Rural Development*. Eds. Konopnicki & Vandevalle. pp 86-90. University of Ghent, ICA, London.

Holdsworth, I. (1980) 'Agricultural Co-operation in Egypt'. In *Review of International Co-operation. Vol. 73, No. 3*, pp 182-199. ICA, London.

Holmén, H. A (1985) 'Comment on the Role of Agricultural Co-operatives in the Rural Development of Egypt'. In *Annals of Public and Co-operative Economy. Vol 56, No. 4*, pp 553-564.

Holmén, H. (1987) 'The Impact of Egypt's Agricultural Co-operatives on Rural Development'. In *Social Change - Journal of the Council for Social Development. Vol. 17, No. 2*, pp 26-34.

Hopkins, N. (1983) *Co-operatives and the Non-Co-operative Sector in Tunisia and Egypt*. Centre for Middle Eastern Studies, Harvard University, mimeo.

Hopkins, N. (1987) *Agrarian Transformation in Egypt*. Westview/Boulder and London.

IADS (1984) *Increasing Egyptian Agricultural Production through Strengthened Research and Extension Programs*. International Agricultural Development Service. ASAID/World Bank/IADS, Arlington VA.

Ibrahim, S.E. (1982) *The New Arab Social Order*. Westview/Croom Helm, Boulder Colorado.

Idris, M. (1986) *Agricultural Pricing Policies and the Role of Farmers' Co-operatives*. CACU, Cairo, mimeo.

Ikram, K. (1980) *Egypt - Economic Management in a Period of Transition*. The World Bank, John Hopkins University Press. Baltimore.

Ismail, M. and Toll, C.J. (1978) *How are the Co-ops? A Survey of the Conditions and Activities of the Local Co-op Societies in Egypt*. ODC, Cairo.

Karlén, L., Åsenius, A., Abbas, H.H., Abd el-Rahman, A. (1984) *Report on the Aid Identification Mission to Agricultural Co-operatives, Egypt*. SCC, Stockholm.

Kirsch, O. (1977) 'Agricultural Co-operatives as an Instrument of Agricultural Policy - Experience with Co-operative Promotion of Production in Egypt'. In *Verfassung und Recht in Übersee*. Ed. Krüger, H. Hamburger Gesellshaft für Völkerrecht und Auswärtige Politik. Hamburg.

Kirsch, O., Benjacov, A., Schujmann, L. (1980) *The Role of Self-Help Groups in Rural Development Projects*. Breitenbach Publ. Saarbrücken/Fort Lauderdale.

Kishk, M.A. (1986) 'Land Degradation in the Nile Valley'. In *Ambio, Vol. 15, No. 4*, pp. 226-230.

Klöwer, G. (1977) *Chansen von Genossenschaften in Entwicklungsländern. Chansen ihrer Entstehung und Chansen als Entwicklungspolitiches Instrument gezeigt am Beispiel Ägyptens*. Phillips Universität, Marburg/Lahn.

Konopnicki, M. (1978) *Introduction, to Co-operation as an Instrument for Rural Development*. University of Ghent/ICA. London.

Korayem, K. (1981) 'The Rural-Urban Income Gap in Egypt and Biased Agricultural Pricing Policy'. In *Social Problems, Vol. 28, No. 4*, pp 417-429.

Lacouture, J. (1971) *Nasser*. Askild & Kärnekull, Malmö.

Leila, A., el Sayed Yassin, Palmer, M. (1985) 'Apathy, Values, Incentives and Development: the Case of the Egyptian Bureaucracy'. In *The Middle East Journal, Vol. 39, No. 3*, pp 341-361.

Mabro, R. (1974) *The Egyptian Economy 1952-1972*. Clarendon Press, Oxford.

Mabro, R. and Radwan, S. (1976) *The Industrialization of Egypt*. Clarendon Press, Oxford.

Marei, S. (1954) 'The Agrarian Reform in Egypt'. In *International Labour Review, Vol. 69 (2)*, pp 140-150.

MEED (1983) *Middle East Economic Digest*. March, July 1983.

Moharram, I. (1983a) *An Historical Analysis of the Agricultural Co-operative Movement in Egypt: 1900-1982*. Economic Working Paper no. 156, Agricultural Development Systems Project, Cairo, mimeo.

Moharram, I. (1983b) *Improving the Role of Agricultural Co-operatives in Egypt.* Agricultural Development Systems Project. Ministry of Agriculture. Cairo, mimeo.

Moharram, I. (1984) *Agricultural Co-operatives and the National Development Plan.* Paper Presented at Symposium: the Future of Co-op Agriculture in Egypt and its Role in Economic Co-operation between Egypt and the Sudan. Cairo, mimeo., in Arabic.

Moore, C.H. (1986) 'Money and Power: the Dilemma of the Egyptian Infitah'. In *The Middle East Journal, Vol. 40, No. 4*, pp 634-650.

Muralt, J. von. (1969) 'Rural Institutions and Planned Change in the Middle East and North Africa'. In *A Review of Rural Co-operation in Developing Areas.* UNRISD, Geneva.

Münkner, H.H. (1983) *The Legal Status of Pre-Co-operatives.* Friedrich-Ebert-Stiftung, Bonn.

Nadim, A. (1979) *The Role of the Village Bank in the Rural Community.* International Islamic Centre for Population Studies and Research. Al-Azhar University, Cairo, mimeo.

Nasr, M. (1983) *Betriebliches Produktionsverhalten im Rahmen des Ägyptischen Systems der Staatlichen Anbauplanung in der Landwirtschaft.* Georg-August-Universität, Göttingen.

Nasser, G.A. (1972) 'The National Charter'. Reproduced in Said, A.M., *Arab Socialism.* Barners & Noble Books, New York, pp 89-133.

Nau, W. (1983) 'Ägyptens Landwirtschaftsgenossenschaften auf dem Weg zu mehr Mitgliederpartizipation'. In *Zeitschrift für das Gesamte Genossenschaftswesen, Band 33, Heft 1.* Vandenhoeck & Ruprecht, Göttingen.

Olsen, G.R. (1976) 'Den Egyptiske stat: Statsinter-ventionismens former og effekter'. In *Politica, no. 2-3, 1976*, Aarhus, pp 82-104.

Radwan, S. (1977) *Agrarian Reform and Rural Poverty, Egypt 1952-1975.* ILO, Geneva.

Rashad, M. (1983) *Towards a new Strategy for Agricultural Co-operatives in Egypt.* el-Taawon Publ. House, Cairo, in Arabic.

Richards, A.(1982) *Egypt's Agricultural Development 1800-1980, Technical and Social Change*. Westview Press, Boulder/Col.

Rodinson, M. (1986) 'The Political System'. In *Egypt Since the Revolution*. Ed. Vatikiatos, P.J., George Allen & Unwin Ltd. London, pp 87-113.

Rydberg, I. (1975) *De arabiska revolutionerna*. Aldus, Stockholm.

SAAD (1982) *Strategies for Accelerating Agricultural Development*. Ministry of Agriculture ARE/USAID.

Sadat, A. (1974) *The October Working Paper*. Ministry of Information/State Information Service. Cairo.

SBW (1986) *Länderbericht Ägypten 1986*. Statistiches Bundesamt Wiesbaden, Verlag: W. Kohlhammer, Stuttgart und Mainz.

Springborg, R. (1975) 'Patterns of Association in the Egyptian Political Elite'. In *Political Elites in the Middle East*. Ed. Lenczowski, G. American Enterprise Institute for Public Policy Research, Washington DC, pp 83-107.

Springborg, R. (1982) *Family, Power and Politics in Egypt*. University of Pennsylvania Press, Philadelphia.

The Egyptian Gazette (1987) March 30.

The Loughborough Statement (1978) In *Co-operatives and the Poor*. ICA, London, pp 19-26.

The Middle East Magazine (1986) January.

The Middle East Magazine (1988) January.

Treydte, K.P. (1971) *Genossenschaften in der VAR (Ägypten) - Entwicklung, Stand und Struktur des Ägyptishen Genossenshaftswesens*. Verlag für Literatur und Zeitgeschehen. Hannover.

UNRISD (1975) *Rural Co-operatives as Agents of Change: a research report and a debate*. UNRISD, Geneva.

Wahba, M. (1983) 'The Egyptian Public Sector: the control structure and efficiency considerations'. In *Public Administration and Development, No. 1, Vol. 3*, pp 27-37.

Wally, Y., el-Kholey, O., Abbas, M., Heady, E.O. (1982) *Strategy for Agricultural Development in the Eighties*. International Development Series, Rep. No. 9. Iowa State University, Ames, Iowa.

Waterbury, J. (1978) 'Egyptian Agriculture Adrift'. In *American Universities Field Staff, No. 47*, pp 1-16.

Waterbury, J. (1983) 'Prospects for Democracy in Egypt'. In *Democracy in Egypt: Problems and Prospects*. Ed. A. Dessouki. Papers in Social Science, Vol. 1, Mon. 2, 2nd ed., Cairo, pp 46-52.

Wertheim W.F. (1972) *Evolution och Revolution. En sociologi för en värld i förvandling*. Rabén & Sjögren, Stockholm.

Yassin, E.S. (1983) 'Social Structure And Democratic Practice'. In Hillal Dessouki, A.E. (1983) (ed.) *Democracy in Egypt: Problems and Prospects*. Cairo Papers in Social Science, Vol. 1, Mon. 2, Cairo.

Young, C., Sherman, N.P., Rose, T.H. (1981) *Co-operatives and Development: Agricultural Politics in Ghana and Uganda*. The University of Wisconsin Press, Madison.

CHAPTER 4

COOPERATIVES IN RURAL DEVELOPMENT IN INDIA
Modern Inputs. Production Structure and Stratification in Sirsi Taluk,
Karnataka State.

By Neelambar Hatti and Franz-Michael Rundquist

THE INDIAN CONTEXT

The concept of cooperation is not in any way new to India[1]. Cooperation, albeit
informally, already existed in ancient times. In its modern form, the cooperative
mode of organization formally owes its origin to the Cooperative Act of 1904,
introduced as a defensive measure for dealing with the problems of rural
indebtedness.

However, the British made no attempts to create a real movement as such. In
the wake of Provincial Autonomy under the Montague Chelmsford Reforms,
cooperation was made a Provincial Subject in 1919, giving options to the
Provincial Governments to have their own outlook and attitude towards
cooperation and assign priorities for its further development. The various
cooperative laws, enacted by Provincial Governments empowered strict
administration and control of cooperatives, a kind of centralized economic
order which was not conducive to the growth of a broad cooperative movement.

The first cooperatives were organized in Kanaginahal and Betagiri in Dharwar
District (in the present State of Karnataka) by a private initiative in 1907.
However, such initiatives were not common during the British period and the
real history of the cooperative movement in India begins with the introduction

---

1. In ancient India there were four forms of cooperation: *Kula, Gramasabha,
Sreni and Jati. Kula* was a social and economic alliance based on kinship.
Gramasabha was a form of cooperation responsible for maintaining economic
and social aspects at village level. *Sreni* was basically an economic organization
of artisans, merchants, agriculturalists and other groups - similar to the
European guild system. *Jati* was a system of cooperation associated with co-
ordination of economic activities of a particular caste or community. Of these
four forms the *Gramasabha* was the most important, since it also represented
the village council and passed through many evolutionary stages (cf. Srivastava
1962).

of planning in the early 1950s, when the cooperative movement was visualized as a vital instrument of economic and social change.

With about 67 million members in 1980, the Indian cooperative movement is among the largest in the world (ICA 1982). Various types of service cooperatives account for 80 per cent of the total membership. The fact that cooperatives cover nearly 95 per cent of all villages also means that cooperatives operate under widely varying local conditions. A prominent feature of the rural areas, in addition to their diversity, is a deep-going social stratification rooted in conditions that seem to reproduce and spread rural poverty.

The Indian Government has repeatedly stressed that a major task of cooperatives is to serve as instruments for *improving the social and economic conditions of the rural poor*[2]. More precisely, cooperatives are expected to reach a large majority of the low-income segments of the rural population with *essential services* such as credit, inputs, consumer goods, processing and marketing of agricultural products. Further, these services are supposed to be provided *efficiently*. In view of the ideological foundations of cooperatives, it should be noted that the movement, through *education* and other means, should efficiently promote members' ability to control their organizations and generally contribute towards improving their *social conditions*.

INTRODUCTION

Rural development efforts have tended to focus on technical aspects, while relatively little attention has been paid to the institutional setting within which development is supposed to occur. Also, in the context of creating and promoting rural organizations, cooperatives in particular, emphasis has primarily been on technical aspects, largely isolated from a broader economic and social context. In the case of cooperatives, it seems to be implicitly assumed that their particular forms of ownership and control by themselves would be sufficient to ensure achievements conducive to social and economic development in rural areas (cf. Gyllström 1988).

Against this background, the present paper[3] attempts, at a micro level, to study whether cooperatives have contributed to the dissemination of improved agricultural technologies and, if so, to analyse the social and economic implications of the process.

---

2. See the various Indian Five Year Plans since 1951.
3. This paper constitutes the second report of a research project entitled *"Cooperatives in Rural Development - Karnataka State, India"*. In turn the research project forms part of a larger research endeavour focusing on the problems of *"Cooperatives and Local Organizations in Rural Development"*.

The analysis focuses on three types of modern agricultural inputs provided by local cooperative societies - fertilizers, hybrid seed and pesticides. The dissemination of these technologies is initially investigated with respect to differential rates of use among cooperative members and non-members. In this context it should be noted that 80 per cent of the landowning households in the study area are cooperative members. Second, the analysis is further refined and differences in household production structures are considered. Here the use of improved agricultural technologies is examined in relation to three categories of household production: paddy only, garden crops only, or a combination of the two. Finally, the analysis focuses on the extent to which the dissemination of improved agricultural techniques relate to the prevailing social and economic stratification of the area investigated.

An earlier paper[4] investigated the relationships between cooperative membership and land ownership in Sirsi Taluk, Karnataka State, India. Findings from this paper clearly show that both land ownership and cooperative membership reflect the prevailing socio-economic stratification through the complex system of castes and sub-castes. A general conclusion from that paper was:

"...as indicated, the cooperatives in Sirsi Taluk seem more geared towards meeting the needs of landowners, particularly those producing garden crops, and, as a consequence of the social stratification, more geared towards serving the needs of the traditionally wealthy and economically powerful groups of the society." (Hatti & Rundquist 1988:13).

The area chosen for the empirical analyses - Sirsi Taluk, Karnataka State - displays interesting variation with respect to its ecological/topographical features and, as a consequence, the ways in which the settlement pattern reflects prevailing social and economic stratification. These factors have been discussed at length in the above mentioned paper (ibid.:2-3), and only an outline of the main features will be given here.

Sirsi Taluk can be divided into three distinct ecological zones (Map 1). The *Western Zone* is dominated by jungles and deep valleys with sandy soils not particularly well suited for the production of paddy or garden crops. The *Central Zone* is made up of broad valleys with fertile loams particularly well suited for the production of garden crops - areca and cardamum. Soils in the *Eastern Zone*, which extends eastward to the Deccan plateau, are generally fertile, consisting of loams and, in the eastern parts of the zone, black soils.

---

4. Hatti, N. and Rundquist, F-M. (1988) *Cooperatives in Rural Development, Land Ownership and cooperative membership in Sirsi Taluk, Karnataka State India*; Department of Social and Economic Geography, University of Lund.

133

Map 1: Karnataka State; zones and sampled Panchayats of Sirsi Taluk

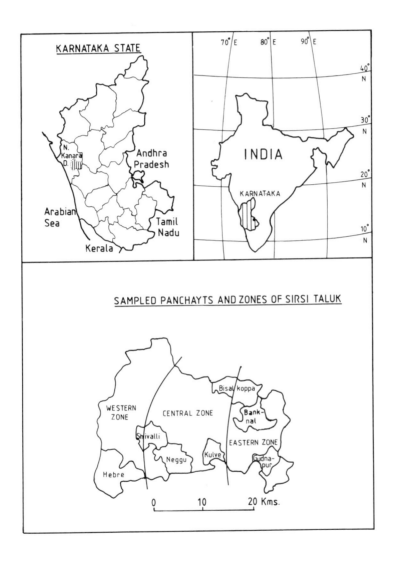

Topographical and soil structure differences generate distinct variations in water retaining capacities and in possibilities for irrigation. In turn, this causes marked local variation in resource bases, and in the profitability of different types of agriculture between the zones.

These variations are also reflected in the settlement pattern of the area. Sirsi Taluk has been settled in a number of successive immigration waves starting in the 17th century and continuing up until the early 19th century. Initially, immigration was dominated by Havyak Brahmins from the coastal areas who settled mainly in the fertile valleys of the *Central* Zone. They initiated labour intensive garden cultivation, which encouraged a second wave of immigration of people from lower castes - Naiks, Kareokkaligas and others - first to the *Central* Zone and later to the *Eastern* Zone. Lastly, the *Western* Zone was settled in the early 1800s by semi-tribal groups, e.g. Kumri Maratis, who migrated from the north (Hatti & Raagaard 1985).

The historical pattern of migration clearly reflects the prevailing socio-economic hierarchy of the Taluk. Brahmins, traditionally of high status, occupy the most fertile areas with highly profitable garden production. Lower castes occupy land more suited for paddy production, which is mainly for local consumption. This social and economic hierarchy is also reflected in the patterns of cooperative membership (Hatti & Rundquist 1988).

Discussions below will initially focus on the issues of data and methodology. Thereafter results of the analyses of the three specific research questions will be discussed under separate headings. Finally, the results are summarized and conclusions are drawn.

DATA AND METHODOLOGY

Data used consists of information pertaining to 2,724 house-holds in Sirsi Taluk. This information was collected through a field survey during January 1980 - June 1981. The households are located in seven randomly selected panchayats. Within each panchayat a universal household survey was conducted (Hatti & Raagaard 1985:4).

Available information at panchayat level is combined into separate data files enabling an analysis at zonal level. In order to achieve this purpose the information for Bisalkoppa panchayat has been distributed between the *Central* and *Eastern* Zones according to village locations (Map 1). Also, in order to avoid too small sub-groups, only the dominant caste or sub-caste groups within each zone are selected and, within these, only landowners are considered. Moreover, based op the Havnour Report (1978), the various castes and sub-castes have been grouped into larger categories. *Brahmins* are treated as a separate category, while Naiks are included in the category *Backward Community*; Kumri Maratis, Kareokkaligas and some other smaller groups are included among *Backward Castes*; finally, Harijans, or the so called casteless people, come under *Scheduled Castes*.

Methodologically, the analysis is pursued by way of subdividing the total population of each zone into sub-groups defined initially by cooperative membership or non-membership. Subsequently, further subdivisions are made according to the acceptance/use of improved agricultural technology, and according to agricultural production structures within the households studied.

The analysis is pursued in steps whereby initially the use of improved agricultural technologies are investigated with respect to cooperative membership. Additionally, the focus is set on identifying differences between the ecological zones of the Taluk, in order to be able to address the question whether distinct differences in the use of improved agricultural technologies can be related to the ecologically defined production structures in Sirsi Taluk.

In a second step the analyses will be further refined, and the use of improved agricultural technology within different caste and income groups will be considered. At the same time the overall analytical approach in considering ecologically determined production structures will be retained.

USE OF IMPROVED AGRICULTURAL TECHNOLOGIES

I. Cooperative membership

The structure of landownership gives an indication of the general economic structure of the areas studied. Table 1 gives information on the overall structure of landownership in the Taluk as a whole, as well as within the three zones defined.

The proportion of landless displays relatively marked differences between the zones. From, in an Indian perspective (cf. Cassen 1982:Ch. 4), a relatively modest ratio of 12 per cent in the *Western* Zone, the figures rise and become as high as 33 per cent in the *Central* Zone. In this respect the *Central* Zone stands out with a markedly higher proportion of landless than the other two zones. It is also obvious that these figures affect the Taluk averages and raise the overall figures of the landless.

The figures, however, reflect agricultural production structures in the Taluk. Agriculture in the *Western* and *Eastern* Zones is predominantly of a subsistence

Table 1: Landless and landowners in the three ecological zones of Sirsi Taluk (percentages within parenthesis).

TALUK/ ZONE	No. of Households	Landless		Land- owners	
SIRSI TALUK	2724	776	(28)	1948	(72)
WESTERN ZONE	211	26	(12)	185	(88)
CENTRAL ZONE	1618	539	(33)	1079	(67)
EASTERN ZONE	895	211	(24)	334	(76)

character. Labour requirements are basically met by the use of family labour. In contrast, agriculture in the *Central* Zone is mainly of a commercial garden production type. Labour needs in the latter type of agriculture are very high. Hence, the high proportion of landless seeking temporary employment on farms producing garden crops (cf. Hatti & Raagaard 1985; Hatti & Rundquist 1988).

The different agricultural production structures, reflected in the landownership pattern, also ought to influence the use of improved agricultural technologies. Table 2 summarizes the use of such technologies in the investigated zones.

At a general level, two conclusions can be drawn from Table 2. First, the use of improved agricultural technologies are related to the predominant production structure. Second, usage varies distinctly with the rate of cooperative membership. More detailed scrutiny of the information, however, reveals interesting variations both within and between zones.

Looking initially at cooperative membership, the relative proportions differ from 57 per cent in the *Western* Zone to more than 80 per cent in the *Eastern* Zone. The figure for the *Central* Zone is slightly lower than 80 per cent. Again, these relationships can be seen as reflections of different production structures and, hence, the perceived advantages for households of being cooperative members. Given the more subsistence oriented types of agriculture in the *Western* Zone, the possible advantages of being cooperative members may not be very strongly felt. In the *Central* Zone, with its commercially oriented agriculture, cooperative membership becomes important in order to secure input supplies. Finally, in the *Eastern* Zone, paddy, although basically for subsistence, is produced on a larger scale and with more intensive techniques than in the *Western* Zone. Cooperative membership is important for securing needed inputs. Membership is also an important factor in securing agricultural

Table 2: Use of fertilizers, hybrid seed and pesticides according to cooperative membership in the three ecological zones of Sirsi Taluk. Land owning households only (percentages within parenthesis).

TALUK/ ZONE/ Coop. memb.	No. land-owning Households	Use of Ferti-lizers		Use of Hybrid Seed		Use of Pesti-cides	
SIRSI TALUK	1933	861	(45)	749	(39)	818	(42)
Coop. memb.	1505	791	(53)	607	(40)	730	(49)
Non-memb.	428	70	(16)	142	(33)	88	(21)
WESTERN	183	30	(16)	143	(78)	53	(29)
Coop. memb.	105	25	(24)	83	(79)	36	(34)
Non-memb.	78	5	(6)	60	(80)	17	(22)
CENTRAL	1069	448	(42)	267	(25)	654	(61)
Coop. memb.	841	417	(50)	218	(26)	591	(70)
Non-memb.	228	31	(14)	49	(22)	63	(28)
EASTERN	681	383	(56)	339	(50)	111	(16)
Coop. memb.	559	349	(62)	306	(55)	103	(18)
Non-memb.	122	34	(28)	33	(27)	8	(7)

production credits, a factor which is most important in the more intensive agriculture of the *Central* and *Eastern* Zones.

Relating cooperative membership more directly to the use of improved agricultural practices generally confirms the inferences drawn concerning underlying motives for membership. At the same time inter-zonal variations in the use of different types of technologies need to be looked into in greater detail. Considering first the use of *fertilizers*, the overall use in the *Eastern* Zone markedly exceeds that of the other Zones. Also, in the *Central* Zone, the proportion of fertilizer users is relatively high - viz. slightly higher than 40 per cent. In the *Western* Zone, however, only 16 per cent of the households use fertilizers. For the *Central* and *Eastern* Zones the figures are clearly related to the more intensive paddy cultivation in both zones, particularly in the *Eastern* Zone. In the case of the *Western* Zone, the low figures reflect adverse conditions for intensive agriculture, and hence the lack of incentives for using improved technologies.

10

Within all three zones, a clear difference in use between cooperative members versus non-members can be observed. Invariably, compared to non-members, a higher proportion of cooperative members use fertilizers. Inter-zonal differences in overall use are retained, however. Among cooperative members the *Central* and *Eastern* Zones display the highest rate of use, reflecting the importance of fertilizers in paddy production. The *Western* Zone is found at the bottom with only about a fourth of the cooperative members using fertilizers. Production structure is also reflected in use among non-members where the rank order is retained among the zones, although at a much lower level.

Hybrid seed use displays a more varied picture than fertilizer use. To an extent, rank order between the zones is reversed in the case of hybrid seed. The *Western* Zone displays the highest rate of use with 77 per cent. Rates of use in the *Central* and *Eastern* Zones are 50 and 25 per cent, respectively. Moreover, use of hybrid seed does not show as clear a relationship with cooperative membership, as was the case with fertilizer use. In the *Western* and *Central* Zones the proportion of hybrid use among members is almost on par with that found for non-members. Only in the *Eastern* Zone does one find marked differences in hybrid use between members and non-members

On the one hand, even though the trends observed are not always consistent, it is possible to infer a relationship between use and the ecologically determined production structure. High rates of usage are found in the primarily paddy producing zones with only a marginal potential for more profitable garden production.

On the other hand, the lack of a consistent trend with a higher proportion of hybrid users among cooperative members, which may have been expected, could be explained by reference to the way in which the cooperative movement functions in Sirsi Taluk. Cooperatives seem more geared towards meeting the needs of land owners, garden crop producers, and the traditionally wealthy (Hatti & Rundquist 1988:13). The relatively high proportion of hybrid use among non-members - frequently being small-scale subsistence paddy producers - can be explained by the fact that cooperatives are not perceived as fulfilling the needs of this group. Consequently, they do not play a major role in influencing adoption patterns for hybrid seed.

Finally, with respect to *pesticide* use, the picture largely resembles that found for fertilizer use. The deviation from the pattern found for fertilizer is that the *Western* Zone has a higher proportion of pesticide use than the *Eastern* Zone, while the opposite was the case for fertilizers. The highest rate of use is found in the *Central* Zone, reflecting production structures and the relationship between the more profitable garden production and use of improved agricultural technologies.

The reversal of rank order between the *Western* and *Eastern* Zones could also be related to ecological factors. On the one hand, climatic and vegetational aspects of the *Western* Zone may be more favourable for insect reproduction and, consequently, make the zone more prone to insect damages on crops. Thus, the incentive to use pesticides should be higher in this zone. On the other hand, given the generally higher prices of fertilizers compared to pesticides, the shift in rank could also be related to economic factors. In Sirsi Taluk, however, the latter are also dependent on the ecologically determined production structures. Consequently, the relationships found could reflect an attempt on the part of *Western* Zone farmers to optimize the use of improved technology in view of their economic constraints.

II. Production structures and cooperative membership

In the above discussion, emphasis was placed on the stratifying role played by land ownership and the use of improved agricultural technologies, linked to cooperative membership. To a large extent the conclusions drawn indicated the underlying importance of ecologically determined differential production structures found in Sirsi Taluk. In order to further clarify the conclusions already drawn, but also as a background to the more detailed analysis of the use of improved agricultural technologies, these differential production structures will be investigated in greater depth.

Table 3 gives information on average agricultural incomes - i.e. total gross *cash incomes* derived from the sale of crops, sale of livestock produce and sale of livestock - according to production structure, cooperative membership and caste affiliation. Production structure has been defined in terms of paddy production only, garden production only and a combination of the two. At this stage no attempts are made to consider the marked variations in land ownership between the different caste groups (cf. Hatti & Rundquist 1988), and, thus, the potential for generating a surplus from agriculture.

At Taluk level, it is clear that the number of households in paddy and garden/paddy cultivation totally dominates. This pattern is reflected in all three zones. With respect to cooperative membership, members clearly dominate among garden and garden/paddy producers, while among paddy producers, the number of members are not equally dominant. In terms of caste affiliations, the proportion of Brahmins among garden and garden/paddy producers is marked, whereas for paddy producers, Backward Community households constitute the largest group. This pattern is also clearly reflected in the distribution of members vs. non-members between different caste groups. In terms of income levels, the dominant position of the Brahmin community stands out as the most striking feature.

Shifting attention to zonal level reveals a number of significant structural inter-zonal differences. First, the large proportion of households engaged in paddy production alone in the *Western* and *Eastern* Zones - 65 and 78 per cent, respectively - compared to only 23 per cent in the *Central* Zone, is noteworthy. Second, the role played by garden production alone in the *Central* Zone stands out as an important feature. To all ends and purposes, the latter type of production constitutes a negligible category in the other two zones.

Concerning overall income distribution, the pattern clearly reflects zonal differences in production structure. It must again be emphasized, however, that the income figures presented refer to *cash* incomes, and do not include subsistence elements consumed within the units of production. Income differentials between paddy cultivators and households engaged in garden production are noteworthy - the incomes generated by paddy cultivators are often well below 10 per cent of those found for garden and garden/paddy producers. If cooperative membership is considered, the differences between the categories become even more pronounced in favour of the producers of garden products.

However, the most interesting aspects concerning the socio-economic stratification generated by the ecologically determined production systems appear at intra-zonal level. In the *Central* Zone the majority of cooperative members are households engaged in highly profitable garden production, and most of these are Brahmin households. Income levels of these households are by far the highest. This is true even for non-members, although at slightly lower income levels.

Among lower castes, Backward Community households engaged in garden production, on the whole, have marginally higher incomes. These households, again, are cooperative members. No Scheduled Caste households are found to be engaged in garden production. Most lower caste households are actually engaged in the less profitable paddy production, and only about 54 per cent are cooperative members.

Agricultural incomes in the other two zones are noticeably lower than those found in the *Central* Zone. Also, the magnitude of these incomes differ markedly between these two zones. Generally, incomes in the *Western* Zone are much lower than those in the *Eastern* Zone. In both zones incomes from garden/paddy production are higher than those from production of paddy alone. A Brahmin dominance with respect to income levels, particularly with respect to garden/paddy production, is also found. Finally, incomes for cooperative members are generally higher than those found for non-members. The latter is particularly evident in the *Eastern* Zone where incomes for both

Table 3: Average *agricultural incomes* according to production structures; cooperative membership and caste affiliation in the three ecological zones of Sirsi Taluk. Land owning households only (No. of households within parenthesis).

TALUK/ZONE Coop membership Caste Affiliation	Paddy only		Garden only		Garden/ Paddy	
SIRSI TALUK						
Coop members	1,066	(589)	8,992	(114)	8,766	(770)
Brahmins	983	(44)	9,696	(96)	11,440	(511)
Backw. Caste	580	(79)	7,716	(3)	2,223	(69)
Backw. Comm.	1,185	(439)	4,744	(15)	3,883	(198)
Sched. Caste	686	(27)	--	--	1,800	(1)
Non-members	353	(263)	6,243	(17)	5,972	(115)
Brahmins	1,294	(28)	8,176	(12)	9,204	(66)
Backw. Caste	122	(62)	--	--	715	(14)
Backw. Comm.	309	(155)	1,603	(5)	1,980	(35)
Sched. Caste	66	(18)	--	--	--	--
WESTERN ZONE						
Coop members	411	(57)	750	(1)	3,818	(43)
Brahmins	742	(20)	750	(1)	6,025	(20)
Backw. Caste	101	(25)	--	--	726	(5)
Backw. Comm.	506	(12)	--	--	2,224	(18)
Non-members	236	(58)	--	--	1,346	(19)
Brahmins	808	(13)	--	--	1,620	(2)
Backw. Caste	37	(27)	--	--	588	(3)
Backw. Comm.	122	(18)	--	--	1,469	(14)
CENTRAL ZONE						
Coop members	692	(126)	9,146	(112)	10,083	(595)
Brahmins	614	(14)	9,894	(94)	11,638	(475)
Backw. Caste	121	(17)	7,716	(3)	2,767	(37)
Backw. Comm	838	(88)	4,744	(15)	4,446	(83)
Sched. Caste	400	(7)	--	--	--	--
Non-members	325	(110)	6,243	(17)	7,326	(88)
Brahmins	1,838	(14)	8,176	(12)	9,753	(61)
Backw. Caste	125	(24)	--	--	632	(9)
Backw. Comm.	105	(67)	1,603	(5)	2,446	(18)
Sched. Caste	0	(5)	--	--	--	--
EASTERN ZONE						
Coop members	1,277	(405)	0	(1)	4,439	(132)
Brahmins	1,979	(10)	0	(1)	12,309	(16)
Backw. Caste	1,115	(37)	--	--	1,526	(18)
Backw. Comm.	1,299	(339)	--	--	3,708	(97)
Sched. Caste	828	(19)	--	--	1,800	(1)
Non-members	457	(95)	--	--	2,070	(8)
Brahmins	0	(1)	--	--	3,099	(3)
Backw. Caste	321	(11)	--	--	1,275	(2)
Backw. Comm.	552	(70)	--	--	1,572	(3)
Sched. Caste	91	(13)	--	--	--	--

paddy only and garden/paddy producing cooperative members are generally higher than those found for non-members.

The highest average income figures are found for garden/paddy producing Brahmins in the *Eastern* Zone. It should be noted, however, that these constitute a group of Brahmins located in Bisalkoppa Panchayat close to the border of the *Central* Zone. With respect to the lower castes the highest incomes are found for Backward Community, although differences between groups are not highly significant.

Comparison of the *Eastern* and *Western* Zones underscores the structural differences discussed earlier. As indicated, overall incomes are generally higher in the *Eastern* Zone. On the other hand, incomes for paddy producers in the *Eastern* Zone are higher than the corresponding incomes found in the *Western* Zone. This pattern is particularly obvious for cooperative members and reflect both the more favourable ecological conditions for paddy production, as well as the partly commercial orientation of this type of production, in the Easter Zone. In the latter case cooperative membership may be particularly important as a means of acquiring essential inputs, as well as providing access to marketing channels.

Summarizing the discussions on Table 3, the impression is one of a markedly economically stratified society. Inter- and intra-zonal income differentials are significant. Two distinct patterns emerge. Inter-zonal variations are manifested through income differentials reflecting the ecologically determined production possibilities of the more profitable garden crops. The *Central* Zone stands out in this respect with overall markedly higher average agricultural incomes than the other two zones. Intra-zonal variations, on the one hand, appear as distinct income differentials between paddy and garden/paddy producers, with markedly higher incomes for the latter group. On the other hand, intra-zonal variations appear as marked income differentials between the different caste groups where Brahmins almost invariably are found at the extreme top of the income hierarchies. Including cooperative membership in the analysis further strengthens the relationships found - cooperative members generally tend to have higher incomes than non-members, while at the same time the caste group differentials are retained. In the analyses below these matters will be further penetrated, and the extent to which the relationships coincide with the use of improved agricultural technologies will be discussed.

III. Use of improved agricultural techniques, production
    structure and cooperative membership

Table 4 indicates the extent to which the use of improved agricultural technologies has contributed to the accentuation of the observed

positions between the caste groups and between members and non-members are retained and further substantiate the earlier findings. On the other hand, use vs. non-use of modern inputs accentuates the stratification in the sense that incomes for the group of non-users tend to be markedly lower than those for users. These patterns, however, become clearer at inter- and intra-zonal levels.

Turning initially to the *Western* Zone, the earlier discussion concerning overall use of modern inputs (Table 2) indicated that the rate of use tended to be lower compared to the other zones. Despite the generally lower levels of income in this zone, however, it is evident from Table 4 that users have higher incomes than non-users. Irrespective of caste, cooperative members using modern inputs have higher incomes. As regards income differentials, Brahmins remain at the top while Backward Caste have the lowest incomes.

In the *Central* Zone, the picture becomes quite different. As discussed elsewhere (Table 2), the rate of use of modern inputs in this zone is relatively high in the inter-zonal perspective. The highest rate of use was found for pesticides, which clearly coincides with the dominance of garden production in this zone. This dominance is further underscored in the income figures presented in Table 4. With the exception of non-member garden/paddy producers belonging to Backward Caste, garden incomes for users and non-users alike are very much higher than those for paddy only producers, particularly in the case of cooperative members. Similarly, among paddy only producers, users of modern inputs tend to have higher incomes than non-users.

Despite favourable conditions for the cultivation of paddy, the income pattern of paddy only producers does not differ significantly from that found in the *Western* Zone. This can be partly explained by the dominance of garden cultivation, which is highly labour intensive, and the high demand for daily wage labour. Such labour is relatively scarce in the *Central* Zone. Thus, paddy only producers, particularly those belonging to non-Brahmin caste groups with low levels of literacy (cf. Hatti & Raagaard 1985), have ample opportunities to supplement their incomes by working in gardens. In case of Brahmins whose literacy levels are much higher (ibid.), the income from agriculture is supplemented by one or more household members working outside the agricultural sector. These aspects will be discussed further below (Table 5).

Finally, the figures for *Eastern* Zone clearly indicate the predominant role of paddy production; almost 80 per cent of the households produce only paddy. With respect to garden/paddy producers the observed pattern is similar to those found in the other two zones - i.e. the general income level is higher, and cooperative members using modern inputs have higher incomes. For paddy producers, however, a qualitative difference is found in comparison with the other zones. This is particularly evident in the generally higher incomes exhibited by cooperative members producing paddy only. Another noteworthy feature, underscoring the importance of paddy cultivation in this zone, is the relatively high level of incomes among cooperative members who do not use modern inputs.

An important aspect underlying the income figures presented in Table 4 is the proportion of agricultural income in the total household income. The emphasis of the earlier discussions has been placed on the role played by differential production structures, and caste-affiliations linked to cooperative membership and use or non-use of modern inputs. It is clear, however, that this may be too narrow a way of identifying critical restrictions facing the different households in their formulation of production strategies. Elsewhere the markedly uneven literacy and landownership patterns at Taluk, as well as at inter- and intra-zonal levels, have been pointed out (Hatti & Raagaard 1985; Hatti & Rundquist 1988). In view of this, it is important to try to capture possible motivational aspects underlying the observed production strategies as these may be reflected in the proportion of agricultural incomes in the total household incomes (Table 5). This table, however, only shows the pattern at Taluk level, as this largely reflects inter- and intra-zonal patterns.

At a general level, in the case of paddy only producers, the proportion of incomes generated from cultivation is less than the corresponding proportion for garden/paddy producers. Further, in the case of paddy only producers, the proportion of agricultural incomes of non-users tends to be lower than that of users. In the case of garden/paddy producers, however, this difference is not as marked. Finally, with respect to cooperative membership, the most noticeable difference is found among paddy only producers - i.e., for members, a larger proportion of the total income is derived from cultivation than for non-members.

The category which is of particular interest here is the paddy only producers since a considerable proportion of their total income is derived from activities other than cultivation. In the case of Brahmins, it is more than likely that the supplementary source of income lies outside agriculture. This is because Brahmins generally have much higher levels of education than other castes, and, as a result, have ample opportunities of obtaining non-agricultural employment (cf. Hatti & Raagaard 1985:89-92). For other castes, however, such opportunities are limited as their levels of literacy tend to be very low (ibid.). In their case, in order to supplement their household incomes, the alternatives available are basically two: to work on a daily-wage basis and/or to intensify cultivation.

As regards intensification of cultivation we have to bear in mind that paddy producers are largely marginal farmers, whose holdings are frequently small and fragmented (cf. Hatti & Raagaard 1985). An attempt to intensify cultivation

Table 5: Average percentage of household income generated from cultivation according to use *(UMI)* or non-use *(NMI)* of modern inputs; cooperative membership and caste affiliation in Sirsi Taluk. Landowning households only.

	Paddy only UMI	NMI	Garden/ Paddy UMI	NMI
Coop members				
Brahmins	51	42	93	92
Backw. Caste	34	34	74	48
Backw. Comm.	62	38	83	78
Sched. Caste	36	21	92	--
Non-members				
Brahmins	66	50	95	89
Backw. Caste	10	11	67	50
Backw. Comm.	41	15	73	46
Sched. Caste	10	8	--	--

under these premises would require a greater amount of labour. A further requirement would be the availability of inputs such as credit, seed and fertilizers. Third, since paddy cultivation is basically rainfed, depending upon the vagaries of monsoon, availability of irrigation sources is essential for an intensification. Even assuming that these preconditions are met, the increase in yield would be such that the additional cash income derived is probably only marginal. As a result, not many farmers are prepared to take the risk and prefer to seek work on a daily-wage basis[5]. This is particularly true in the *Central* Zone where the predominance of garden production provides many opportunities of obtaining such work for up to five months per year. In fact, the additional cash income obtained from chosing a strategy of daily-wage labour would markedly exceed that generated from intensified cultivation (ibid.).

In the context of the possibilities of intensified cultivation we have to consider the role of local cooperative societies. It has been pointed out that the societies are primarily geared towards meeting the need of larger landowners, particularly garden owners (Hatti & Rundquist 1988). Thus, even if paddy cultivators were willing to make efforts to improve cultivation, the present

---

5. According to Epstein (1967), the economic rationality of Indian farmers regarding risk aversion in physical and economic environments of uncertainty is based on average productivity and not marginal productivity.

structure of local societies acts as a constraint in the sense that it provides unequal access to the necessary inputs.

CONCLUSIONS

The foregoing analysis generates a distinct impression of a markedly economically stratified society where income differentials are significant. First, these reflect the ecologically determined production structures. Second, income differentials between castes are substantial, Brahmins almost invariably at the top of the income hierarchy. Third, cooperative members tend to have higher incomes than non-members, while caste-group differentials are retained.

Our analyses further show that users of modern inputs have higher household incomes than non-users. While this is true for both cooperative members and non-members, members using modern inputs generally have the highest incomes. One explanation for this differential has to do with access to modern inputs and credits provided by local cooperative societies. In terms of caste affiliations, Brahmins using modern inputs have the highest average household income. Among the other castes, relative positions between caste-groups are retained. Here again the explanation has to be seen in terms of access. Brahmins, with their traditionally stronger economic and social position, tend to dominate the local cooperatives and, as such, can utilize more effectively the services provided. Moreover, when local societies are unable to meet the requirements of the Brahmin farmers, their strong economic position enables them to buy the needed inputs on the open market.

Finally, the analyses show that the role played by local cooperative societies in the dissemination of modern agricultural technologies differentiates between the type of production structure and caste affiliation. The groups that tend to benefit are cooperative society members whose incomes are already relatively high, i.e. primarily garden/paddy crop producing Brahmins as compared to paddy only producers, who mainly belong to lower caste-groups. Thus, it is evident that cooperatives in Sirsi Taluk exacerbates these inherent inequalities.

LITERATURE

Cassen, R.H. (1982) *India*: Population, Economy, Society. Macmillian, London.

Epstein, S. (1967) 'Productive Efficiency and Customary System of Rewards in Rural South India'. In Firth, R. (ed.): *Themes in Economic Anthropology*, Tavistock, London.

Gyllström, B. (1988) *State Administered Rural Change*. Agricultural Cooperatives in Kenya. Cooperative Research Programme, Department of Social and Economic Geography, University of Lund, Lund.

Hatti, N. and Raagaard, S. (1985) *Agricultural Labourers and Small Cultivators, A study in Sirsi Taluk, Karnataka*. Centre for Development Research, Copenhagen.

Hatti, N. and Rundquist, F-M. (1988) *Cooperatives in Rural Development*, Land ownership and cooperative membership in Sirsi Taluk, Karnataka State, India. Department of Social and Economic Geography, University of Lund.

Havnour Commission Report (1978) Government of Karnataka, Bangalore.

ICA (1982) *Statistics of Affiliated Organizations*, Comparative Statement 1979-80. International Cooperative Alliance, Geneva.

Srivastava, G.P. (1962) *Traditional Forms of Co-operation in India*. New Delhi.

13. Migration in Sweden. A Symposium. Edited by *Hannerberg, D., Hägerstrand, T.* and *Odeving, B. (1957)*.
14. *Kulldorff, G. (1955)* Migration Probabilities.
15. *Ajo, R. (1955)* An Analysis of Automobile Frequencies in a Human Geographic Continuum.
16. *Ahlberg, G. (1956)* Population Trends and Urbanization in Sweden 1911-1950.
17. *Godlund, S. (1956)* Bus Service in Sweden.
18. *Godlund, S. (1956)* The Function and Growth of Bus Traffic within the Sphere of Urban Influence.
19. *Nordström, O. (1958)* Pendelwanderungen in die Industriorte in Südschweden 1750-1955. Eine Studie über die Möglichkeiten der Fabriken die Reservarbeitskraft des Umlandes auszunutzen.
20. *Hannerberg, D. (1960)* Schonische «Bolskiften».
21. *Godlund, S. (1961)* Population, Regional Hospitals, Transport Facilities, and Regions. Planning the Location of Regional Hospitals in Sweden.
22. *Eldblom, L. (1962)* Quelques points de vue comparatifs sur les problèmes d'irrigation dans les trois oasis libyennes de Brâk, Ghadamès et particulièrement Mourzouk.
23. *Törnqvist, G. (1962)* Transport Costs as a Location Factor for Manufacturing Industry.
24. Proceedings of the IGU Symposium in Urban Geography, Lund 1960. Edited by *Norborg, K. (1962)*.
25. *Grytzell, K.G. (1963)* The Demarcation of Comparable City Areas by Means of Population Density.
26. *Morrill, R. (1965)* Migration and the Spread and Growth of Urban Settlement.
27. *Pred, A. (1967)* Behaviour and Location. Foundations for a Geographic and Dynamic Location Theory. Part I.
28. *Pred, A. (1969)* Behaviour and Location. Foundations for a Geographic and Dynamic Location Theory. Part II.
29. *Brown, L.A. (1968)* Diffusion Dynamics. A Review and Revision of the Quantitative Theory of the Spatial Diffusion of Innovation.
30. *Törnqvist, G. (1968)* Flows of Information and the Location of Economic Activities.
31. *Illeris, S.* and *Pedersen, P.O. (1968)* Central Places and Functional Regions in Denmark. Factor Analysis of Telephone Traffic.
32. *Eighmy, T.H. (1968)* Problems of Census Interpretation in Developing Countries: The Western Nigeria Case.
33. *Grytzell, K.G. (1969)* County of London. Population Changes 1801-1901.
34. *Grytzell, K.G. (1970)* Methods for Demarcation of Cities Compared.
35. *Törnqvist, G. (1970)* Contact Systems and Regional Development.